"Dudley employs a vivid and highly readable prose style, ... the bulk of [which] will likely make for invigorating reading for fellow devout Christians."

— *Kirkus Reviews*

I am unique,
just like everyone else
in the world.

The Bridge of Hearts
Building Trustworthy Connections

Johnny L. Dudley

Edited by Leigh Westin
Illustrated by Terre Britton

CONSECRATED **PRESS**

Dedication

This book is dedicated to my wounded brothers and sisters in Christ, those precious people who have been humbly decorated with God's Purple Heart.

And to Bobby Basset, my lifelong friend, and his precious daughter Holly.

The Bridge of Hearts: Building Trustworthy Connections

Published by Consecrated Press LLC
Jacksonville, Florida, US 32258

ISBN 978-1-7351900-1-3
eISBN 978-1-7351900-0-6

Dudley, Johnny L. 1950–
© 2020 Johnny L. Dudley

The Team: AQ editor: Leigh Westin
Interior design: Terrabyte Graphics
Cover Graphic: Digital Juice, Inc.
Cover Design: Terre Britton

Printed in the United States of America

First Edition 2020

1 2 3 4 5 6 7 8 9 10

Table of Contents 🍃

Dedication _____ i

Acknowledgments _____ ix

A Letter to the Reader _____ xi

Section I—My Story: The human heart can be unpredictable and self-centered, contrary to the nature of God. Therefore, our nature must be changed to be compatible with him. _____ 1

    1 The Grocery Cart Story _____ 3
    2 Returning Excellence _____ 9
    3 The Valley of Baca _____ 13

Section II—The Human Story: There are two seeds for two kingdoms—*the kingdom of man* and *the kingdom of God*. By looking at the first seed, we can see why a second seed was necessary to prepare us for the kingdom of God. _____ 19

    4 The Story of Adam _____ 21
    5 The Creation of Eve _____ 27
    6 Eternal Fertilization _____ 33
    7 Two Adams, Two Seeds, Two Kingdoms _____ 41
    8 Known Unto God _____ 45

Section III—Her Story: A gospel record tells of a heart being changed. _____ 49

    9 The Alabaster Box _____ 51

Section IV—The Hidden Mystery: There was a mystery hidden in the heart of God from before the world was—a mystery that was undisclosed to man until God's appointed hour. The riches of this mystery are more precious than gold. _____ 55

10 Treasure Hunters _____ 57

11 The Mission Statement _____ 63

12 Obtain or Become_____ 67

Section V—The Spiritual Connection: Our natural world has many cycles to sustain the wonders of life: the cycle of the sun, the cycles of the moon, and the cycles of the rivers. But there is an even greater cycle in the spiritual world, a live-giving cycle that must be cultivated, nurtured, and carefully protected to sustain the joy of life. _____ 73

13 The Cycle of Life_____ 75

14 The Secret Place _____ 81

15 The Wall _____ 87

16 The Ministry of Reconciliation _____ 93

Section VI—A Blueprint for the Bridge: God has established both natural and spiritual laws to govern our universe. His natural laws govern temporary things, but his spiritual laws govern eternal things. It would be wise to learn them both. _____ 99

17 Clear and Pointed Instructions _____ 101

18 The Law of Love _____ 105

19 The Heavenly Pattern _____ 113

20 The Pattern's Three Dynamics _____ 121

21 The Pattern's Seven Steps_____ 129

22 Validating the Pattern _____ 135

Section VII—Building the Bridge of Hearts: The human heart does not sit still; it is either building emotional walls or spiritual bridges. Building a spiritual bridge is like building any structure; it begins with a first step and ends with a last. _____ 141

23 Step One: Spiritual Attraction_____ 143

24 Steps Two and Three: The First Dynamic _____ 151

25 Steps Four and Five: The Second Dynamic _____ 159

26 Steps Six and Seven: The Third Dynamic _____ 167

27 The Seven Spirits of God_____ 181

Section VIII—The Pattern's Forerunner: The blood of animals could not change our nature. It couldn't take away our sins, heal our hearts, or impute God's righteousness to us, so God prepared a very special man to make this sacrifice for us. Now the onus is on us to put our faith in the blood of this man. _____ 187

28 The Compounded Gift _____ 189

29 The Blood Covenant _____ 195

30 Preparing the Lamb_____ 201

31 Sealing the Covenant _____ 209

Section IX—A Finished Work: God's blessing for everlasting life is on unity with him and others, which explains why he gave us the pattern for spiritual reconciliation. Once its requirements are met, there is no need for further reparation. _____ 215

32 The Joy of Unity _____ 217

33 Justice _____ 221

34 Chronicles_____ 227

35 Stopping the Bleeding_____ 233

A Song of My Life _____ 239

About the Author _____ 241

About the Publisher_____ 243

Endnotes _____ 245

We were not built to just receive love, hoard it, or self-direct it, we were built to give love. God's love must flow into our hearts and out of our bellies as rivers of living water, or we will stagnate within and die.

Acknowledgments 🌿

The best illustration I can give is, I sent Leigh Westin a hundred pounds of steel wool and asked her to weave me a Volkswagen. The original work I sent to her was beyond disorganized. Had it not been for the last seven years of Leigh's extraordinary patience and perseverance, this book could have never been finished. But through her very capable and faithful editing, she not only led me to the finish line, but she has also become a deeply trusted friend. Thank you, Leigh, thank you very much.

I must also thank Terre Britton, founder and owner of *Terrabyte Graphics*, for her long-standing patience and talent in creating the cover design, illustrations, website design, and marketing strategies. She, too, brought her heart to the table and put it into this work.

I'd like to also thank Joe Ort for his major contribution of personal time, counsel, and the encouragement I needed to press on. Thank you, Joe.

I'd also like to give special thanks to Daniel Ward, Nancy Quatrano, Gail Albritton, and Anne Evans for their valued contributions.

A Letter to the Reader 🍃

Dear Reader,

I am not a minister in the strictest sense of the word, nor do I hold a degree in theology, but I've spent most of my life studying the Bible. I am seventy years old at the completion of this writing and have studied the Bible almost daily, hours before the sun, even when I didn't follow its counsel and foolishly did things my way.

I was not called to go to a seminary, but I was called to study. The apostle John told us the Spirit of God is our teacher (see 1 John 2:27); the apostle Paul told Timothy to study and show himself approved unto God to become a laborer who rightly divides the word of truth (see 2 Timothy 2:15). So I took Paul's counsel to heart and began to study.

When I sought a private tutor in my midtwenties, my goal was to glean what he had learned and build from there. Having served the church as a pastor and teacher since he was sixteen years old, Pastor Archie Smith had studied and taught the Bible for more than seventy-five years. I learned many good things from my gentle friend and his faithful wife, a very notable one being, "There are a lot of good books in the world and you can't read them all, so only read the best." Following his line of thinking, I have endeavored to write the best book I could write about God's objective in creation and what Christ has done to make it our reality.

The Bridge of Hearts may challenge some long-standing religious traditions, so I have documented its claims with biblical chapters and verses for references. *My intent is to tell you, not to sell you*, to provide you, the reader, with a basic insight into God's most significant goals for humankind so you can make informed decisions. I hope to provide a clear vision of the Bible's most fundamental truths, which are: God loves us with a perfect love that's always just, always merciful, always grace filled and, even more important, *always focused on us*. In turn, his objective is to teach *us* how to return his love from a heart that's always just, always merciful, always grace filled and, even more important, *always focused on him*.

The goal is unity—spiritual unity—that we may be one with God and our neighbor through the same spirit that makes God the Father one with God the Son—the Holy Spirit. To accomplish this highest goal, our Father has provided us with two immensely powerful tools for building spiritual connections: the first is his Ten Commandments that define the goal, and the second is his simple diagram for meeting the goal—the pattern.

> My intent is to tell you, not to sell you.

The pattern God gave the world through Moses is the heart and soul of this book, because it's God's blueprint for building spiritual bridges between living souls. It's the only diagram he ever gave to show all men how to approach the holiest place of his heart for communion and, if it works for God, it will work for those he's made in his image.

I've included a few short stories about my personal experiences for illustrative reasons, but I've written this book to be a tribute to the works of God through Jesus Christ. It's about *what* Jesus has done to build our spiritual connection with God, *how* he has done it, and *why* he has done it for us—about how he was broken for us to make us all of one Spirit, God in us, and us in God.

This book is about hope. And I hope everyone reading this book will gain a deeper insight into God's incredible promises submerged in Scripture and find the hope we all need for life. It may require some time and work—perhaps a lot of work, but please, let patience have its perfect work. The Bible has promised God will reward all of those who *diligently* seek him.

I also hope you enjoy reading *The Bridge of Hearts* and find it rewarding. If you do, please visit your favorite book site and post a review or visit my website and leave a comment on consecratedpress.com. And even if you don't, I hope you'll send me an email and let me know your thoughts.

Johnny

Section I—My Story

I have come to the conclusion that
this age knows almost everything about life
—except how to live it.

It's not enough to know about life,
we must know how to live life.

KATHRYN KUHLMAN
A GLIMPSE INTO GLORY

1

The Grocery Cart Story ✒

The heart is deceitful above all things,
and desperately wicked: who can know it?

JEREMIAH 17:9

The human heart is an enigma, a paradox of contradictory qualities. There are times when we feel our hearts are completely trustworthy and times when we wonder if our hearts can be trusted at all. Based on my experience, I've found my heart can be inconsistent and unpredictable. This appears to be a common dilemma for many of us. We can feel the warmth of love and still not perform it.[1] But God, who is rich in mercy, has promised to change our nature and make us eternally reliable if we will heed his call and accept the invitation to his table of honor.[2]

That ye may eat and drink at *my table in my kingdom.* (Luke 22:30, italics added)

God's invitation is attended by a precious gift of clemency called grace, and it's through grace that we are accepted at his table. And as we shall see in the coming chapters, God's grant of clemency has been offered to every man, woman, and child on earth because of the faithful acts of one man, Jesus the Christ.

Being justified freely by his grace through the redemption that is in Christ Jesus. (Romans 3:24)

I am growing old and my time is short, so I am passing on what I have learned through a lifetime of study and observation. I do not wish to sell you anything, but I would like to tell you what I've learned through almost fifty years of studying the Bible and reading many books by Christian authors, so you, too, can make informed decisions about the incredible hope that God has set before us. I wish to tell everyone who will listen why God's grant of clemency is the most precious gift he could've ever given to us.

Thanks be unto God for His indescribable gift. (2 Corinthians 9:15)

> ...what I really wanted all along was total self-indulgence without any negative consequences.

There are multitudes in every generation who have closed their ears to the gospel's message and chased unbridled fancies to their imagination's vanishing point. I'm ashamed to admit it, but I'm guilty of this charge. If I could tally my lifelong actions with complete and accurate data, I'm afraid the bottom line would show that what I really wanted all along was total self-indulgence without any negative consequences. But that hasn't worked too well for me.

To the best of my recollection, the first telltale sign of my self-centered nature was revealed in one of the strangest of places—a grocery cart. I have two amusing grocery-cart stories, but this one stands out as one of the first shallow-water markers in my navigation through life.

Mom was careful to keep the cart just far enough away from the candy shelf to thwart my very determined reach. So when my high-pitched sobs resulted in serious threats from the one who had said she loved me, the only remaining option I had was to climb out of that grocery cart at the first opportune moment and take this important matter into my own little hands.

I can still see the cashier's blurry silhouette as I bolted past the checkout counter and out the front door at the lightning speed of my five-year-old legs. It seemed at the time my safest haven to gorge on chocolate plunder—and hide from Mom's impending wrath—was the floorboard in the back seat of our second-hand Chevrolet.

As is typical, judgment took a while, but it still came swifter than I wanted, that is, if I'd even considered the consequences at all. Back then, I was convinced it was all Mom's fault. I'd have been devoid of any negative consequence if she had simply agreed with what I wanted and purchased the candy.

The five-minute ride home in deafening silence afforded the much-needed time to consume most of those chocolate delights from the beautifully colored bag. It was not enough time, however, to cool the intense fervor of an embarrassed mother's wrath.

Looking back, it's hard to believe she allowed me to finish those stolen chocolates, but she did, and I wasn't sure why. What I now know through hindsight is, she had other plans.

I will never forget the impending doom in her stern look. Quaking in fear behind the living room couch, I defiantly landed the last M&M on the top of my tongue. To my recollection, it was then that I first learned how the fleeting pleasures of self-indulgence could bring serious consequences.

From my cornered perspective behind the couch, the huge belt in her right hand seemed as big as any nuclear weapon known to man. And because my only resource for strategic planning had been the mind of a five-year-old child, I had failed to plot an exit strategy. I was cornered, seriously doomed, hopelessly condemned, and we both knew it. It would take many hours of my extended sobbing and crying for her indignation to pass so she could tell me again that she loved me. Once her wrath had passed, my thoughts returned to those succulent chocolates with the crunchy nut centers and the day when I'd get some more.

Proverbs 22:15 says, "Foolishness is bound in the heart of a child; but the rod of correction shall drive it far from him." In hindsight, I'd have to say our heavenly Father knows all about the foolishness in the heart of a child and the rod of correction since he has children too—us. We are born again as the children of God, but not as the mature men of God. So I believe it is safe to say that most of us have set our jaws like flint and insisted on having our way at the candy shelf of life. This is certainly true of me.

As I grow older, I can see that becoming a mature man in the likeness of Christ is the finish line, not the starting line.[3] I can also see that self-indulgence has been my clandestine goal from my youth, even after calling on the name of the Lord for salvation.[4] My natural proclivity toward selfish choices has been my most challenging nemesis, but it has also been one of my best teachers.

> ...becoming a mature man in the likeness of Christ is the finish line, not the starting line.

It took me through perilous places that made me so hungry and thirsty for the righteousness of God that I temporarily exchanged my world for a few years of seclusion in the Rocky Mountains. Pulling my travel trailer some eighteen hundred miles to Colorado, I set up my camp above ten thousand feet, so I had a place to live while building a small timber cabin in the fall and winter of 2010. I knew I needed to change my surroundings to renew a right spirit within me. At sixty years of age, I could not shake the lingering awareness that I'd been following the prodigal[5] instead of the forerunner.[6]

Blessed are they which do hunger and thirst after righteousness:
for they shall be filled.

MATTHEW 5:6

I press toward the mark for the prize of the high calling
of God in Christ Jesus.

PHILIPPIANS 3:14

And he that taketh not his cross, and followeth after me,
is not worthy of me.

MATTHEW 10:38

2

Returning Excellence 🍃

Our works are not about earning God's love,
they're about returning God's love.

JOHNNY L. DUDLEY

'm not a Rocky Mountain man, just a Florida boy, but I love those Rocky Mountains where circumstances led me to spend a number of years in quiet contemplation—where I learned something about what it means to surrender my will and follow Christ.

I had purchased a tract of land about two miles above sea level five or six years before I had a purpose for its use—or so I thought. Little did I realize when I acquired the land that God, who has always been faithful to me, was preparing my way to become faithful to him. Therefore, when I had my first clashing encounter with some mischievous little terrorists called chipmunks, my heart was virgin territory for a divine lesson.

Much like God's love for us, I just can't help but love these impish little troublemakers. I suppose that's why I have made daily donations of black oil sunflower seeds to their purely selfish cause. Now my little buddies have multiplied to such great numbers, they've become a bit of a challenge, testing my patience by getting into everything I wish they wouldn't. There are so many of those naughty little seed burners surrounding my cabin, even my best efforts to keep them from eating my expensive store-bought flowers have become mostly futile.

The little rascals bring back memories of the old Donald Duck and Chip and Dale wars on Disney. Worst of all, if I fail to feed them in a timely fashion, they'll stand on their little hind legs, flick their fuzzy tails, and give scolding chipmunk chirps of impatient demands for their breakfast seeds. I amusingly suspect that sooner or later they might band together and overpower me, taking every seed I have in a chipmunk coup d'état.

I'm glad our heavenly Father uses nature to teach me about my relationship with him and others, as is the case with these impish little creatures. I've often learned through observation that, much like my not-so-humble self, my militant little subjects want immediate gratification yet never stop to give thanks or even to acknowledge me, the one who has provided for them. Woe is me.

This may sound a bit childish, but it kind of hurts. Deep down inside I wish they'd come to me, hop on my lap, and let me hold and pet them. I'd just like for them to return the same level of affection I give, without fear or selfish motives, but they don't. In fact, they don't even seem to comprehend it is I who feeds them and that I care. What's puzzling is, they're very smart, yet they act as if they don't trust me or even want to be bothered with returning my love. Still, when they want something from me, oh boy, they'll lift their panhandler eyes in a prayer-like gaze and demand immediate sustenance. Once they get what they want, the little bandits run away to their own dark corner of the world, under some rock, woodpile, or old tree stump, until their greedy little bellies want something more. It never occurs to them that true protection and the joy of fellowship could be derived from returning my love.

Unfortunately, in time a weasel came along and began to wipe many of them out. It was kind of like Judgment Day for the chipmunks.

I suppose there's actually very little comparison between a chipmunk and a human being, except they both have street smarts and are very creative creatures with panhandler eyes. But my experience with these rebellious little mortals has given me great cause to reflect on those deeply felt words of Jesus the Christ when his heart lamented over Jerusalem.

O Jerusalem, Jerusalem, you who kill the prophets and stone those sent to you, how often I have longed to gather your children together, as a hen gathers her chicks under her wings, *but you were not willing.* (Matthew 23:37, NIV, italics added)

Our heavenly Father wants us to consistently return his love on the same level he gives it. He wants to engage with us in a life-giving connection that's built on the three underlying dynamics of love—faithfulness, truth, and trustworthiness. Could we even suspect the Creator of the heavens and earth who has created all things for his pleasure[7] would settle for anything less than for us to return his love in the same way he gives it?

God is love, and what we are about to explore is that he is developing the same strength of his love in us so we can be one with him. Wouldn't it be reasonable to assume that if we returned his love as he gives it, he would overshadow us, protect us, and give us the precious seeds of his words of life? Of course, he would! If I can love chipmunks that I neither foreknew nor created, how great is our Father's love for us? John wrote, "Herein is love, not that we loved God, but that he loved us, and sent his Son to be the propitiation [atoning sacrifice] for our sins" (1 John 4:10).

It embarrasses me sometimes when I stop to think about how many times I have cried out to God in times of need, much like a pudgy-cheeked chipmunk, then when my belly was full, I went my own way and sought the cover of darkness. I have been *unfaithful* to him even though he has always been *faithful* to me. Much like those furry little bandits, once I got what I wanted, I'd run off to some dark corner of the world and indulge myself at the candy shelf of life until I wanted something more. It's no wonder David lamented over the foolishness he found in his own heart.

So foolish was I, and ignorant: I was as a beast before thee. (Psalm 73:22)

We all want the benefits of God's love to flow from his heart to ours like a river of living waters. We want to have those benefits available on demand like tap water from the kitchen sink at our beck and call in our times of want or need. The truth is, we can have these benefits if we are willing to meet God's two simple requirements—yield our will and faithfully follow our forerunner. Our forerunner's way is narrow, but he will lead us through our valleys of tears where we will learn to love like our Father loves, because our Father first loved us.

We love him, because he first loved us.

1 JOHN 4:19

Behold, what manner of love the Father hath bestowed upon us, that we should be called the sons of God.

1 JOHN 3:1

He that loveth not knoweth not God; for God is love.

1 JOHN 4:8

3

The Valley of Baca 🍃

Blessed is the man whose strength is in You,
Whose heart is set on pilgrimage.
As they pass through the Valley of Baca,
They make it a spring;
The rain also covers it with pools.
They go from strength to strength;
Each one appears before God in Zion.

PSALM 84:5–7, NKJV

meq ha-Baka, or *Baca*, in Hebrew means "valley of the weeper."
The valley of Baca is the valley of the weeper where we are
taught the value of love. Our journey through this valley can be
unbearable at times, but in hindsight, I can see it's the most beautiful
valley for developing children. It's where we grow from the child of
God to the man of God who, in the likeness of our heavenly Father,
becomes faithful, true, and trustworthy.

Baca is where the seeds of love and deep compassion are prospered
in the souls of those who have struggled to yield their will and turn
their faith toward God.[8] Just as thorns from the stem of the rose will
pierce the skin, the pain and sorrow of Baca will pierce the heart,
causing tears to fall like driving rains. But tears are crucial to every

person's survival, because tears are needed to learn about both sides of love—the joy and the sorrow. So tears are good—excellent tools in the hands of a Master Craftsman. They form refreshing pools in our valleys of sadness to reflect the glory of God from deep within us.

The strength obtained in our valleys can become a wellspring of life in those who turn their hearts toward God and overcome their insufferable defeats.[9] Many who pass through this valley will grow from strength to strength until they appear before God in Zion. They may stumble and fall under Baca's burden, and those who fall will be broken,[10] yet no one must stay there—no one. Jesus gave us God's promise in writing when he said, "Come unto me, all ye that labour and are heavy laden, and I will give you rest" (Matthew 11:28).

This book is a little bit about me, some of my crushing valleys and mountaintop experiences, but it's mostly about what our Father wants to do in the hearts of everyone who's hungry and thirsty for righteousness. I will be sharing a few excerpts from my life's story to certify my own need for our Savior, but quite frankly, I'm challenged with feelings of caution. Do I attempt to keep my skeletons neatly tucked away in a closet where they are hidden from public view, or should I be plainspoken and vulnerable to the potential backlash of those who have never sojourned through the valley of tears?

If I choose to be vulnerable, I know some of the colors in my character portrait will be telling and dark, embarrassing to paint. On the other hand, if I hide behind a mask of religious pretense, I'm even more afraid of becoming just another whitewashed sepulcher who might look good on the outside, but on the inside is full of dead men's bones.[11] So I have made a compromise. I have chosen to be somewhat vulnerable and transparent, to tell the truth without all the ugly details.

My Valley

I learned a lot about courage in Vietnam where I spent a year of my life in what we called the bush, where I learned that *courage* is not the same as *spiritual resolve,* maybe not even close. Courage is for a moment, but resolve is daily, every day, all day long —resolve is by far the greatest courage, and I believe it is probably the greatest challenge that faces us all. True resolve requires a personal determination to choose to love when its requirements oppose our will, a choice I have found to be difficult but rewarding.

I like being loved, but I don't always like the requirements for returning love. I've found returning love is much harder than being loved because it is not always in concert with my will. So I have a history of using every resource in my arsenal of personal talents to secure love's benefits from the hands or hearts of others without incurring the cost, that is, without consistently returning their love. That hasn't work too well for me. It led me deep into the valley of Baca but never to the Promised Land.

> Courage is for a moment, but resolve is daily, every day, all day long.

> It led me deep into the valley of Baca but never to the Promised Land.

My journey through Baca began many years ago, after fellow church leaders confronted me about some improper actions. So I painfully resigned and left the people I loved. The world of business wrote the next few chapters of my life. I didn't attain the status of many businesspeople, but I did acquire enough assets through real estate investments to become ensnared in the monotony of having too much money and too much spare time.

Working together, they steered my lifelong quest for fulfillment into some very stormy waters.

Business was never truly my home due to my ongoing study of Scripture, but neither was the church my home due to my evolving lifestyle. I felt distant from both worlds, like the man without a country. Taking a hard-left turn from my previous life into the maze of worldly attractions,[12] I followed the steps of the prodigal son and tackled my boredom with similar pleasures.

> The deterioration of a man's character is something he seldom sees coming—it can be as subtle as the erosion of a rock.

The deterioration of a man's character is something he seldom sees coming—it can be as subtle as the erosion of a rock. Even when others who loved me saw what was happening and tried to help, I denied the truth and reacted defensively. God, however, can use the sands of time to put true grit into a man's gut.

Deep down inside there was a growing awareness of my personal deterioration that was spotlighting my need for change. I knew I was walking on thin ice, but it seemed I couldn't change even if I wanted to—and I wasn't sure I wanted to. So I wandered in and out of self-indulgence until a crushing defeat took my soul into the valley of the weeper, where, after years of struggle and pain, a joy began to blossom from the ashes of the sacrifices I finally made.[13]

I began to pray for God to change me. I suppose what I really wanted him to do was zap my heart and instantly change my nature with little to no effort of my own, but God doesn't work that way for many of us. He seldom takes the difficult challenges out of our lives, because he uses those challenges to develop our strength and overcome our weaknesses. Our heavenly Father wants us to develop the same heartfelt resolve for righteousness that exists in Christ, so we can follow his Son out of our valleys and return God's love with singing.[14] God's heart-transforming work can be arduous and painful and incredibly slow by my standards,[15] but if we endure through the night, there is joy in the morning.[16]

Thou tellest my wanderings: put thou my tears into thy bottle: are they not in thy book? When I cry unto thee, then shall mine enemies turn back: this I know; for *God is for me.*

PSALM 56:8–9, ITALICS ADDED

When God wants to do an impossible task,
He takes an impossible man and crushes him.

ALAN REDPATH

It is doubtful whether God can bless a man greatly
until He has hurt him deeply.

A. W. TOZER

Section II—The Human Story

But what man, in his natural condition, has not got,
is Spiritual life, the higher and different sort of life
that exists in God.

C. S. LEWIS

4

The Story of Adam 🌿

And the Lord God formed man of the dust of the ground, and
breathed into his nostrils the breath of life;
and man became a living soul.

GENESIS 2:7

The human story begins with Adam, the first living soul in a body
of flesh. His story, told in Genesis, reveals the great desire that
existed in God before he created our human race, his longing for
intimate communion. By breathing his desire into the heart of Adam,
our heavenly Father has provoked all people to seek and attain that
which cannot be attained without it—the joy of unity. According to
King David's 133rd Psalm, unity is key, it is where God has commanded
the blessing, even life for evermore.[17]

The importance of unity is further supported by God's first and
second commandments. They call us to unity with God and our
neighbor through the highest possible standard of love—with all we've
got. By linking God's first two commandments to love with the 133rd
Psalm about unity, it becomes readily apparent that God's blessing for
eternal life has everything to do with creating and maintaining unity.
Adam proved this to be true a long time ago when he breached the
joy of Eden by defiling his relationship with God.

Had Adam been ready and able to meet the divine requirements for an unblemished connection with God's Spirit, he would've been able to maintain the joy of unity and sustain his life, but he wasn't able to do this. He wasn't able to faithfully return God's standard of love. Had he been, Adam would've never violated his relationship with God, and he would have accepted the full responsibility for his bride's disgrace by laying down his life for hers, as did Christ, but Adam didn't do this. He didn't have the mind and heart of Christ who willingly gave his life for ours. On the contrary, he threw both God and Eve under the bus in a desperate attempt to justify himself, saying, "The *woman* whom *thou* gavest to be with me, *she* gave me of the tree" (Genesis 3:12, italics added).

> God's blessing for eternal life has everything to do with creating and maintaining unity.

It is important to note, Eve was deceived by the serpent (see Genesis 3:13), but "Adam was not deceived" (1 Timothy 2:14). Adam simply made a choice to exalt himself and then, when he was confronted, he blamed God and Eve for his actions. Adam showed his hand when he proved he was willing to justify himself at their expense. When he did, he broke the most basic precepts of life and love called faithfulness. As a result, Adam was driven from the face of God.[18]

Adam's story confirms a most basic truth: faithfulness is the antonym of self-centeredness. It confirms that the joy of love is lost when unity is broken, and unity is broken when faithfulness is broken. His story

> Adam showed his hand when he proved he was willing to justify himself at their expense.

shows us that this highest and most rewarding experience of life called unity is only sustained through a deep and intimate spiritual connection that is built with faithful, true, and trustworthy hearts. Our spiritual

...faithfulness is the antonym of self-centeredness.

connections with God and others must go deeper than what is found through mere *physical* or *intellectual* contact, they must be built on the deepest resolve of the divine nature called faithfulness.

Thy faithfulness reacheth unto the clouds. (Psalms 36:5)

Whereby are given unto us exceeding great and precious promises: that by these ye might be partakers of the divine nature. (2 Peter 1:4)

When God breathed his life into the dust and gave his breath to Adam, he passed his yearning for unity to Adam's conscious awareness. Our Creator God breathed his emotional longing so deep into Adam's core consciousness that it continues to channel through our hearts today. So Adam was given life and longing, but he was not yet given the mind and heart of Christ that Peter identified as the divine nature. Therefore, Adam was callow and carnal, a self-centered man with a selfish nature who was unable to meet God's spiritual criterion for an everlasting life through unity.

Adam was too young and inexperienced to understand the importance of faithfulness. God's word had not been sent and the nature of Christ had not been formed within him.[19] So Adam didn't fully comprehend the beauty of faithfulness—that to faithfully love from the heart is the way of life in our Father's kingdom. So let's take a closer look at the first Adam's story, because there's so much more to this amazing narrative than what initially meets the eye.

The Creation of Adam

God's longing was genetically passed to Adam's heart through his breath, his *Neshamah,* which in Hebrew means "his spirit, vital breath, divine inspiration, innate consciousness." Once we grasp the Genesis record that our longing for unity was passed from God's heart to ours, we will begin to understand that God's longing for unity is at least in part, if not entirely, what prompted his desire to create us.

> God's longing for unity is at least in part, if not entirely, what prompted his desire to create us.

Revelation reminds us that God created all things for his pleasure.[20] This would certainly include our human race. Through Adam, God has created a kingdom of natural men and women who would share his longing for spiritual unity but would not be able to consistently uphold their longing to God's righteous standard until the divine nature of Christ was formed within them. To me, this makes perfect sense, because from before the beginning, God ordained us to be created in Christ Jesus.

For we are his workmanship, *created in Christ Jesus* unto good works, *which God hath before ordained that we should walk in them.* (Ephesians 2:10, italics added)

For God to give us his eternal longing and then walk us through Baca with Christ as our Shepherd makes a whole lot of sense to me. It's how he's chosen to teach us the importance of faithfulness before we receive our incredible inheritance. I believe these difficult experiences in our valleys will propel us to the highest level of life and love when Jesus restores us to the face of God.[21]

> ...from before the beginning, God ordained us to be created in Christ Jesus.

These things have I spoken unto you, that my joy might remain in you, and that your joy might be full. (John 15:11)

God gave Adam his longing in Eden, but Adam didn't complete his spiritual development in Eden. Had he done so, Adam, like Christ, would have never been unfaithful or thrown his Creator and bride under the bus.[22] Our forefather Adam was created in God's three-person image of a tangible body, a conscious soul, and the spirit of man, but unlike Christ, he was not given the Spirit of God without measure (see John 3:34)—not yet. The bottom line is, God gave Adam his longing in Eden, but the strength to fulfill his longing would not be complete until the nature of Christ was formed within him, until he was created in Christ Jesus.

And ye are complete in him, [Christ] which is the head of all principality and power. (Colossians 2:10)

My little children, of whom I travail in birth again until Christ be formed in you.

GALATIANS 4:19

Whereby are given unto us exceeding great and precious promises: that by these ye might be partakers of the divine nature.

2 PETER 1:4

Marvel not that I said unto thee, Ye must be born again.

JOHN 3:7

5

The Creation of Eve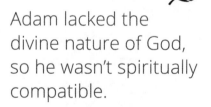

For Adam was first formed, then Eve.

1 TIMOTHY 2:13

Before the creation of Eve, Adam felt alone. His relationships with animals had left him somewhat disconnected and dissatisfied, so he was lonely (see Genesis 2:18). Adam was created for spiritual intimacy at the highest level of life and love, the divine level, so neither the beasts in the field nor the fowl of the air were able to satisfy his deepest emotional needs. Animals were different from Adam, so he couldn't find that rewarding union of beings he yearned for in his heart.[23] Although his longing for spiritual intimacy had come from God, it wasn't found with God either—not yet. Adam lacked the divine nature of God, so he wasn't spiritually compatible.

> Adam lacked the divine nature of God, so he wasn't spiritually compatible.

Adam was not yet prepared for the highest union of beings with the highest being of all—the Most High God. He couldn't be one with God in an unblemished spiritual connection, because he was a corruptible creation.[24] Adam was designed to be corruptible for a very important reason, so he could be implanted with the seed of God's Spirit to form the nature of Christ within him (see 1 Corinthians 3:16, James 1:21). Therefore, Adam, his bride, and the ongoing generations of his natural descendants were held on the outside of God's heart by an emotional wall called a veil until they were made partakers of the divine nature. So Adam felt lonely.[25]

And the Lord God said, it is not good that the man should be alone. (Genesis 2:18)

Adam felt love for God in his heart, and God certainly loved Adam, visiting him in the cool of the day to walk and talk with him[26] for face-to-face communion. But Adam's love for God proved to be conditional, it was more like a natural bond of *phileo* love. He had the feelings of warmth and affection that accompanies a brotherly love, but he lacked the depth of love our Messiah would plunge to by giving his life for ours—agapao love—the depths of love a person would die for.[27] Had Adam been willing and able to meet the divine requirements of *agapao* love in Eden, he would've yielded his will to God's and resisted sin, even unto the shedding of his own blood. In the likeness of the Christ who was yet to come, he would've given his life for his bride's, but Adam didn't do this.

> Had Adam been willing and able to meet the divine requirements of agapao love in Eden, he would've yielded his will to God's and resisted sin, even unto the shedding of his own blood.

Adam had a strong affection for God and Eve, but he wasn't faithful from his heart and our omniscient Creator knew it. He knew Adam would violate trust on his very first temptation, because he knew

Adam lacked the conviction to love like he loves. For this reason, God kept the veil before the holiest place of his heart to protect his heart from Adam and the generations of his seed until we would be completed in Christ. If Adam had been qualified to enter God's holiest place and become spiritually connected with the Spirit within, he would have been our forerunner instead of Christ—and, of course, Adam would have never been lonely.

Whither the forerunner is for us entered, even Jesus. (Hebrews 6:20)

The Temporary Solution

Adam was lonely because he wasn't a completed man who could sustain a faithful connection. He was incapable of sustaining God's moral code of conduct and soaring with his Creator to the highest level of life and joy through the faithful performance of an unblemished love. Therefore, our omniscient Creator provided a temporary solution for Adam's loneliness and ours, until Jesus, the divine seed should come[28] and conform us to his image. Paul confirmed this when he wrote to the Roman church, "For whom he [God] did foreknow [us], he also did predestinate *to be conformed to the image of his Son*, that he might be the *firstborn among many brethren*" (8:29, italics added). And then again to the Colossian church he wrote, "Christ in you, the hope of glory" (1:27). If Christ, the Word made flesh, is the firstborn of many brethren, then Adam, the firstborn of the human race, was not like him.

Adam was certainly a unique creation, possessing the character traits of both genders in one man, the masculine and the feminine. This is made evident in the Genesis story of Eve's creation. She was taken out of Adam, from out of his side,[29] so the character traits of both genders apparently existed in Adam before she was taken from his side and *the one was made two*—male and female.

If we were to examine Scripture, we would soon discover how all the character traits that are commonly assigned to each gender, including the *power of the masculine gender* and the *wisdom of the feminine*, are character traits existing in God. It appears these traits were passed from God's heart to Adam's, through God's breath, before Eve's was taken out of him.

To keep Adam's story straight, we need to remember that our Father's true objective was way beyond the creation of just one man, our Father wanted a family.[30] He wanted a pure and holy people who actively returned his standard of love from the heart with his same unwavering conviction—a beloved family who could soar with him to the highest level of life and love through the joys of spiritual unity. So Adam was never allowed to eat from the tree of life as a corruptible living soul. God had plans to form the nature of Christ in him and many of his descendants to make them incorruptible before they could eat from the tree of life and live forever (see Revelation 2:7).

Christ in you the hope of glory. (Colossians 1:27)

God's time in the garden with Adam was never intended to last forever. Eden was merely a glimpse into glory, a foretaste of what our relationship with God will be like, once the nature of Christ is formed within us and Jesus presents faultless before the presence of our Father's glory.

My little children, of whom I travail in birth again until Christ be formed in you. (Galatians 4:19)

The Importance of Eve

Both God and Adam had a purpose for Eve. Adam needed Eve to comfort his loneliness, and God created Eve to propagate our race. So God caused a deep sleep to fall on Adam and divided the one man into two genders by taking the female genetics from out of the man.[31] She was taken from Adam's side to be his soul mate, comforter, and a temporary solution for the loneliness in his heart until Christ could be formed within them and they both could become one with the Father through the endless ages to come. Temporary, because they would only be husband and wife until the day they were parted through the death of their natural bodies, for in the coming resurrection there will be neither male nor female, but all will be one in God with Christ (see Galatians 3:28).

So God made Eve from Adam's rib, a natural female from the natural genetics of the first natural man. Eve was given the spirit of man like Adam, to make her a compatible and soothing helpmate. This division of genders gave them the compatible nature they needed to walk as one and comfort each other throughout their season of growth until they fulfilled their destiny together.

> God made Eve from Adam's rib, a natural female from the natural genetics of the first natural man.

Like Adam, Eve was a corruptible living soul with talent, emotion, ambition, intellect, and a moral code of conduct that was very much like his. She was created to be his soul mate, a compatible spirit who could share in his various levels of physical, intellectual, and emotional contact. As such, Eve not only shared the same manner of body, soul, and spirit, she also shared the same deep-seated yearning for the joy of unity. Then, in due time, the two genders became one flesh and bore the offspring we are today.[32] Out of the one came two, and then the two became one.

> Out of the one came two, and then the two became one.

Eve was not of greater or lesser worth than Adam, she had equal value with different strengths. How brilliant was God to utilize half of Adam's humanity to create a magnetic soul mate who could placate his longing until their creation was completed in Christ Jesus and they were restored to the face of God with faultless hearts.

Now unto him that is able to keep you from falling, and to *present you faultless before the presence of his glory* with exceeding joy.

JUDE 1:24, ITALICS ADDED

For now we see through a glass, darkly; but then *face to face*: now I know in part; *but then shall I know even as also I am known.*

1 CORINTHIANS 13:12, ITALICS ADDED

But as it is written, Eye hath not seen, nor ear heard, neither have entered into the heart of man, the things which God hath prepared for them that love him.

1 CORINTHIANS 2:9

6

Eternal Fertilization 🍃

Having been born again, not of *corruptible* seed [flesh]
but *incorruptible* [word], through the word of God
which lives and abides forever.

1 PETER 1:23, NKJV, ITALICS ADDED

While addressing the men of Athens, Paul made a very bold and exacting statement, declaring, "We are the offspring of God" (Acts 17:29, NKJV). To be called God's offspring is an extraordinary concept that more deeply pinpoints the essential truth—we must be born again. We must be begotten again of God's spiritual seed to have his divine nature formed within us. For me, this provides a deeper insight into our spiritual standing with our heavenly Father. Becoming someone's offspring means to be born from the combined seeds of both parents. In the case of becoming God's offspring, we must be born again by combining the spiritual genetics in the seed of God's word with the natural genetics in the seed of man's flesh, as was Christ, the firstborn of many brethren.

The Word was made flesh and dwelt among us. (John 1:14)

I like to think of God's word as the seed of his spiritual genetics, because it is his word in us that reproduces his Spirit in us. The Adam from Eden was God's son through the creation of his tabernacle of flesh (see Luke 3:38), but Jesus the Christ is God's Son through the procreation of his Spirit in the tabernacle—the first begotten Son.[33]

God is a Spirit and his word is his spiritual seed.[34] Therefore, it was the union of the spiritual seed of God's word with the natural seed of Mary's flesh that put the Spirit of God in Jesus's flesh without measure (see John 1:14, 3:34). In like manner, it is God's word in us that reproduces his spiritual genetics in our minds and hearts to prepare us for eternal compatibility with him.

> God is a Spirit, his nature is love, and his Spirit is the life in our Father's heart as well as the life in his Son's heart, so these three are one.

When James wrote, we must receive with meekness the engrafted word to save our souls, he was *not* speaking about the restoration of the same corruptible human spirit, the spirit of man, that existed in Adam before he was corrupted—heaven forbid. He was speaking about the birth of a new man—an incorruptible man—a new creature in the likeness of Christ.[35] James was talking about men and women who were implanted with the seed of God's word to develop the higher ways of God's mind and heart within them. Paul called this new mind "the mind of Christ" (1 Corinthians 2:16).

God is a Spirit, his nature is love, and his Spirit is the life in our Father's heart as well as the life in his Son's heart,[36] so these three are one.[37] It's because the third person of the Holy Spirit lives and abides in the Father and the Son that they are one spirit, and it's why the seed of God's Spirit must be implanted in us to make us one with them in his eternal kingdom. This union of God's seed with man's flesh is presented in all four gospels as a marriage analogy of Christ, the bridegroom, with his church, the bride.

The Marriage Analogy

He that hath the bride [the church] is the bridegroom [Jesus Christ]. (John 3:29)

In times past, when I've considered this marriage analogy as it relates to our union with Christ, I've often experienced a slight discomfort with being called the bride of Christ—perhaps it's a male thing. Now, however, I see the portrait more clearly and perceive the beauty of what is being said. The analogy of Christ and his bride is about the union of two seeds, the *incorruptible seed* of God's word, with the *corruptible seed* of man's flesh. It's about Christ in us.

Christ in you, the hope of glory. (Colossians 1:27)

Two Radically Different Seeds

The apostle Peter gave us a very clear and pointed insight into these two radically different seeds for procreating God's offspring when he told us one is corruptible and the other, incorruptible. Peter calls the first, or natural, seed of our flesh *phthartos*, which means it is "corruptible, it can be impregnated and changed by seeds of thought called words." Words can be seeds of truth or seeds of deception that bring life or death to living souls. He then calls the second, or spiritual, seed of God's word *aphthartos*, which means just the opposite, it is "incorruptible and imperishable."

> "The living soul is corruptible, it can be impregnated and changed by seeds of thought called words."

God's word of truth "lives and abides forever" (1 Peter 1:23, NKJV); therefore, it's his word in us that puts the immortal life of his Spirit in us.

Our living souls were designed to be corruptible, so our hearts could be implanted with God's word of truth to procreate his Spirit within us. But this corruptible design of the soul has a dark side that presents us with another option that sparks our freedom of choice. Being corruptible makes us subject to a lethal form of corruption called deception. The living soul can be impregnated and changed by the seeds of truth that Jesus called wheat or the seeds of deception Jesus called tares (see Matthew 13:24–30). God's word of truth brings life and godliness, but the tare is the seed of erroneous thought that makes us susceptible to contamination and ruin, because it perverts rational thinking.[38] Like a virus, these seeds of erroneous thought bring a spiritual affliction to the soul that deceives and destroys the heart from within.[39] I call this spiritual affliction the *sin virus*.

> Being corruptible makes us subject to a lethal form of corruption called deception.

> For sin, taking occasion by the commandment, deceived me, and by it killed me. (Romans 7:11, NKJV)

The life in the corruptible seed of man's flesh is mortal, and the life in the incorruptible seed of God's word is immortal; the seed of the flesh dies in time, but the seed of the Spirit never dies. Never.[40] God is love, his word is truth, truth is his spiritual seed,[41] and his truth abides forever. Paul gives record that God puts "this treasure [the seed of his Spirit] in earthen vessels, that the excellence of the power may be of God and not of us" (2 Corinthians 4:7, NKJV), "that no flesh should glory in his presence" (1 Corinthians 1:29).

The Natural Illustration

Paul also told us the invisible things of God are clearly seen through his natural creation.[42] One of the best illustrations of God's invisible things is found in the natural reproduction of human beings. It is common knowledge that our natural reproduction requires the union of two different seeds— male and female gametes—a corruptible ovum and an incorruptible sperm. An ovum is corruptible because it can be penetrated and fertilized by the male sperm, but a sperm is not corruptible because it cannot be penetrated or fertilized by the female ovum. The corruptible seed of the ovum, or female gamete, must be implanted or fertilized with the incorruptible seed of the sperm, or male gamete, to become one new life—a new creature—a human zygote.

> Both seeds have life before they are joined as one, but they cannot retain their life and fulfill their purpose unless they are joined as one.

Both seeds have life before they are joined as one, but they cannot retain their life and fulfill their purpose unless they are joined as one. The two seeds must be merged to preserve their life and accomplish their most perfect work.

So I must ask, "Is the process of spiritual reproduction different from that of natural reproduction?" It is not. A closer look at what occurs when two human seeds are joined to propagate a natural life provides deeper insight into what occurs when God's word is joined with man's flesh to propagate a spiritual life. God's immortal word must be merged with man's mortal flesh to preserve his life and accomplish God's most perfect work.

Man is corruptible, God is not; man changes, God does not change (see Malachi 3:6). When the incorruptible gamete of

God's spiritual word is implanted in the corruptible heart of a living soul, the two seeds become one new life and the person is changed.[43] God's seed impregnates and fertilizes the heart of the person's soul with the spiritual genetics of his divine nature to propagate his Spirit within us.[44] I call this process *eternal fertilization*. Ultimately, this divine process will transform a person's thoughts, convictions, and actions into the likeness of God's to form their indelible nature.

So we see a parallel between natural and spiritual reproduction. In human reproduction, the female gamete is initially a form of corruptible life that can be penetrated and implanted with the life in the male gamete. In like manner, our living souls are initially a form of corruptible life—much like the female ovum, they can be penetrated and implanted with the incorruptible life in the seed of God's word.

Words are seeds of thought. They act as spiritual gametes that reproduce their concepts in our minds, which once received and believed, are implanted in our hearts to become our new reality—our new man. The new thoughts they produce in our minds and hearts will ultimately recreate our nature, manage our choices, and redirect our actions.

Once eternal fertilization is accomplished in our souls, we are born a second time by God's Spirit of life.[45] The divine embryo is then hosted in our temporary tabernacles of flesh to be nurtured, developed, and ultimately resurrected from the dust as a mature person in the stature and fullness of Christ.[46] John wrote, when we see him, we shall be like him as told below.

Beloved, now are we the sons of God, and it doth not yet appear what we shall be: but we know that, when he shall appear, *we shall be like him*; for we shall see him as he is. (1 John 3:2, italics added)

A Final Thought

For many are called, but few are chosen. (Matthew 22:14)

It has been reported that the average American couple births between two and three children during their lifetime. Although our human bodies produce an enormous number of seeds, most just cycle and die because they were never joined to become one new life. If the individual male and female gametes are merely mortal seeds that cycle and die like flowers in the field unless they are joined,[47] then a living soul who has never been fertilized by the spiritual gamete of God's immortal word will also cycle and die. How could two mortal seeds from two mortal beings reproduce immortal life? They cannot, they do not. Mortality does not reproduce immortality. Only eternal fertilization by God's immortal word can reverse our natural digression from life to death to the spiritual progression of death to life—temporary life to eternal life, mortality to immortality.

> How could two mortal seeds from two mortal beings reproduce immortal life? They cannot, they do not. Mortality does not reproduce immortality.

Verily, verily, I say unto thee, Except a man be born again,
he cannot see the kingdom of God.

JOHN 3:3

So when this corruptible shall have put on incorruption, and this
mortal shall have put on immortality, then shall be brought to pass the
saying that is written, Death is swallowed up in victory.

1 CORINTHIANS 15:54

Ye also are builded together for an habitation of God
through the Spirit.

EPHESIANS 2:22

7

Two Adams, Two Seeds, Two Kingdoms 🌿

And so it is written, The *first man* Adam was made
a living soul; *the last Adam* was made
a quickening [life-giving] spirit.

1 CORINTHIANS 15:45, ITALICS ADDED

There are two Adams—two seeds for two kingdoms. The first was the seed for the kingdom of man,[48] the last, the seed for the kingdom of God.[49] The man from Eden was the first Adam; the man from Bethlehem is the last. The man from Eden was a living soul; the man from Bethlehem is a life-giving spirit. The first Adam was the union of God's breath with the dust; the last was the union of God's word with the breath.[50] The first was created with the spirit of man;[51] the last was born of the Spirit of God.[52] The first was corruptible; the latter, incorruptible.[53] The first, created;[54] the latter, begotten.[55] The first, carnally minded with a focus on self; the last, spiritually minded with a focus on others.

The first Adam was a living soul in a tabernacle of flesh; the last Adam was God's word in the tabernacle—a life-giving spirit. The first was created for the habitation of God through the Spirit;[56] and the last was given the Spirit without measure.[57] The first Adam was commissioned to be fruitful, multiply, and replenish the earth with a brotherhood of living souls (see Genesis 1:28). The last was commissioned to secure a brotherhood of life-giving spirits from among those living souls—the church.[58] Paul confirmed this order of development for the persons created in Christ when he wrote, "The spiritual did not come first, but the natural, and after that the spiritual" (1 Corinthians 15:46, NIV). Both Adams were foreknown of God from before the foundation of the world,[59] and both are seeds for different kingdoms with a predetermined role in the development of God's offspring.[60]

> The first Adam was merely a type of the last.

For whom he did *foreknow,* he also did *predestinate* to be *conformed* to the image of his Son, that he [Jesus] might be the firstborn among many brethren. (Romans 8:29, italics added)

Again, the first Adam was corruptible because he was created to be implanted with the seed of God's word for *eternal fertilization.* Jesus made this very clear when he said we must be born again (see John 3:7); and James made it clear when he wrote, "Receive with meekness the engrafted word, which is able to save your souls" (James 1:21). The first Adam was merely a type of the last.

A Type of Christ

Who [the first Adam] is a type of Him who was to come [Jesus the last Adam]. (Romans 5:14, NKJV)

The first Adam was a type of Christ. The Greek word *typos* that is translated as *type* in the above passage means "example, fashion, figure, pattern—a prototype." A prototype is something that exhibits the essential or basic features of a later type. This was true of the first

Adam. He exhibited the essential or basic features of the last, but he was not a completed man in the stature and fullness of Christ. Accordingly, he didn't have a strong conviction to uphold a faithful defense against the fiery darts of erroneous thought.[61]

A prototype is something that exhibits the essential or basic features of a later type.

Again, Adam would not be a completed man until he was perfected into the stature and fullness of Christ.

> Till we all come in the unity of the faith, and of the knowledge of the Son of God, unto a perfect man, unto the measure of the stature of the fulness of Christ. (Ephesians 4:13)

The First Adam

The story of the first Adam bears a strong similarity to one of the most memorable experiences of my life—the day I took my first solo flight. As a student pilot, I'd acquired about seven hours of flight instruction when my instructor believed I was ready for the big step. As I taxied my little airplane onto the runway, alone for the very first time, I was intoxicated with exhilaration. The day had finally arrived when I was realizing one of my greatest dreams. As I eased the throttle forward, engulfing the sound of my beating heart in the deep-throated growl of the engine, the earth fell from beneath my feet and the heavens became my destiny.

Three times I lapped the field, landed, and took off again. Each time I passed my instructor, he waved me on from where he stood beside the asphalt runway. My instructor knew what I felt, having been there himself, and he shared in the joy of my triumph. I was born into the world of flight that day, but it was only the first phase of becoming an accomplished pilot, not the final objective. Although I had obtained my wings and could fly a simple airplane, I lacked the depth of understanding and reliability that's forged in the fires of time through the hammers of experience and the tutelage of a faithful instructor. Like my forefather Adam, I was a solo pilot, not an accomplished aviator who was fully prepared to traverse the high places—yet I longed to go there.

My little children, of whom I travail in birth again
until Christ be formed in you.

GALATIANS 4:19

Christ in you, the hope of glory.

COLOSSIANS 1:27

They which are the children of the flesh [Abraham's or Adam's seed],
these are not the children of God.

ROMANS 9:8

8

Known Unto God 🍃

I am God, and there is none like me, Declaring the end from the
beginning, and from ancient times the things that are not yet
done, saying, My counsel shall stand,

and I will do all my pleasure.

ISAIAH 46:9–10

n the book of Acts, Luke wrote, "Known unto God are all his
works from the beginning of the world" (15:18). Given that
the Lamb of God was slain from the foundation of the world (see Revelation 13:8), this foreknowledge of God's would certainly include the creation of our human race, its subsequent fall, and the fullness of our redemption. The Bible tells us

> ...the first Adam was given the spirit of man, not the Spirit of God.

that God created man for spiritual unity with himself, from deep to deep, so we could be one with him (see John 17:21). But what the Bible never tells us, not even once, is the first Adam was ready for a divine correlation of spirits with God while he was a callow living soul in Eden—it never says Adam was one with God or that he possessed God's divine nature. Again, the first Adam was given the spirit of man, not the Spirit of God. The last Adam would be the first flesh to be given the Spirit of God without measure (see John 3:34)—the firstborn of many brethren (see Romans 8:29).

God could've sown his seed in the first Adam's heart, and he could've protected him from the fiery darts in Eden. He could've even let him eat from the tree of life and live forever under his divine protection, but he obviously chose not to. In the likeness of Christ who was made perfect through sufferings,[62] Adam and his natural seed were designed to be implanted with the engrafted word and strengthened through the winds of adversity, so that as God's paternal offspring, we would be strengthened in the inner man by the might of his Spirit (see Ephesians 3:16). God's ultimate objective being, that we would be the heirs of God and joint heirs with Christ, so we could all be glorified together.[63] Therefore, even before the fall of Adam, God had already purposed a full recovery of innocence for those he foreknew and predestined to be conformed to the image of his Son. God is a family planner, and his plan was to call them, conform them, justify them, and glorify them. He even numbered the hairs of our head.[64]

> For whom he did foreknow, he also did predestinate to be conformed to the image of his Son, that he might be the firstborn among many brethren. Moreover whom he did predestinate, them he also called: and whom he called, them he also justified: and whom he justified, them he also glorified. (Romans 8:29–30)

God *created* the first Adam to take us into the valley of Baca, and then sent the last Adam to lead us out. Our omniscient Father knew the first Adam would be corruptible before he breathed life into the dust and placed the created man in Eden (see Genesis 2:8), which is why the Lamb was purposed to be slain before the world was (see

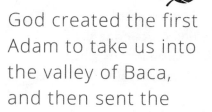

> God created the first Adam to take us into the valley of Baca, and then sent the last Adam to lead us out.

Revelation 13:8). And God knew the natural man and his seed would remain corruptible until the nature of Christ would be formed within them. He knew the first Adam was not even close to being ready for the huge challenge of faithfully returning his love. And, of course, Adam soon proved God was right.

A Recap of Adam and Adam

As we have seen, the first Adam proved he wasn't accomplished in love and couldn't be trusted. His unfaithfulness proved beyond all doubt he couldn't meet love's requirements when those requirements opposed his will.[65] But the last Adam was worlds apart from the first. Jesus traversed the high places of God, with God, long before he created all things for God[66] and long before he was sent to redeem us. But the first Adam never even got off the ground before he crashed and burned.

God wasn't taken by surprise as if something unexpected had spoiled his plan—perish the thought. Like a doting father over a precious son, he'd already made provisions for the first Adam's fall before the foundation of the world (see Revelation 13:8). His plan was to restore us to innocence through the faithfulness of the

> His plan was to restore us to innocence through the faithfulness of the last Adam, so we could walk out of our valleys and traverse the high places with experienced hearts that were determined to love.

last Adam, so we could walk out of our valleys and traverse the high places with experienced hearts that were determined to love.

Our heavenly Father had no intention of restoring the first Adam or his descendants to the lower level of phileo love they had shared in Eden. He had much greater plans. He was after a holy and beloved people who could soar with him through the highest pinnacles of agapao love, the depths of love a soul would die for.[67]

Much like new solo pilots, the natural generations of the first Adam were never intended to soar those high and lofty places of life and love without the nature of Christ being formed within them, which is why our race was never allowed to eat from the tree of life and live forever (see Genesis 3:22). We must eat the bread of life from the last Adam (see John 6:48) before we can eat from the tree of life with those who overcome. This ancient report deserves our most careful attention.

To him that overcometh will I give to eat from the tree of life, which is in the midst of the paradise of God. (Revelation 2:7)

Now this I say, brethren, that flesh and blood cannot inherit the kingdom of God; neither doth corruption inherit incorruption.

1 CORINTHIANS 15:50

For to be carnally minded is death;
but to be spiritually minded is life and peace.

ROMANS 8:6

Now he that hath wrought us for the selfsame thing is God,
who also hath *given unto us the earnest of the Spirit.*

2 CORINTHIANS 5:5, ITALICS ADDED

Section III—Her Story

There is no pit so deep that God's love is not deeper still.

CORRIE TEN BOOM

9

The Alabaster Box 🍃

And, behold, a woman in the city, which was a sinner...brought an
alabaster box of ointment.

LUKE 7:37

t might have been a cool, clear day at the home of Simon the Pharisee
where Christ, his disciples, and a group of others assembled for
dinner. During their gathering, a socially scorned, apparently fallen
woman unexpectedly entered the room with a small container that
was intricately carved from alabaster.

The delicate mineral was beautifully fashioned, and the quality
of the workmanship gave the stone container a certain value in its
own right. But the true value of the woman's offering was not the
cherished container, rather it was the costly ointment sealed inside.
While those in the room were startled by her bold and uninvited
entry, they were even more amazed at her next emboldened act. She
proceeded to break the beautiful box and pour the valuable spikenard
onto the feet of Christ, releasing the precious ointment, and filling
the room with its sweet and aromatic fragrance (see Luke 7:37–50).

Alabaster is of little value, being simply a mineral that's workable
in the hands of a craftsman. Once carved, however, the stone can
become a beautiful work of art, most precious to its rightful owner.

The woman had cherished the finely crafted box until that notable day when its glory was broken to release the costly ointment sealed inside, and only by being broken did it yield its place of fleeting significance to the savory aroma of its precious outpouring.

It's the same with man. Like the alabaster box, our bodies are temporary containers made of dust, tabernacles of flesh designed by our Creator to be filled with that most precious ointment of his Holy Spirit.[68] Dust is of little value, except to be workable in the hands of a craftsman. God is the craftsman, the master craftsman, who has taken that most ignoble portion of matter and sculptured our bodies into glorious works of art.[69] And though our flesh is only a temporary container, it's been our cherished possession from the day of our birth.[70] Our bodies have been beautifully fashioned with intricate designs and have value in their own right, but once God's Spirit is born within us, the glory of our flesh will begin to be broken until it yields its place of fleeting significance to the savory aroma of God's precious outpouring from within us.

The Spirit gives life; the flesh counts for nothing. (John 6:63, NIV)

He that believeth on me, as the scripture hath said, out of his belly shall flow rivers of living water. (John 7:38)

Now, the name of that fallen woman is uncertain, and there has been a lot of controversy over who she really was. Some believe she was Mary Magdalene from whom seven devils were cast out,[71] while others believe she was the sister of Martha.[72] Some believe she was neither of these women, and some believe she was both. The general consensus, however, is she was a prostitute, a woman publicly disdained in the eyes of society.[73] But who she was or where she had been is not nearly as important as where she was going—as what was happening in the secret place of her soul.

Something spiritual was occurring deep in the core of her being, beyond the wall that protected her heart from the hurtful darts of social scorn. Something so spiritually precious that it caused her to cast all caution to the wind and expose her soul to the ridicule of society's elite. Perceiving the Spirit of God in Christ, she'd come face to face with the divine nature and was humbled and broken by the holy encounter. True humility is forged within when we perceive our darkness by the light of God's holiness.

> **True humility is forged within when we perceive our darkness by the light of God's holiness.**

In that precious moment of spiritual release, the woman's wall fell. The emotional veil that had safeguarded her heart from social scorn was torn from top to bottom and the seed of God's Spirit was implanted within, sparking his light of life. Then, releasing her love in the highest expression of adoration, the woman poured out her soul without reserve and returned God's love with unshackled praise, filling the room with that sweet and aromatic fragrance of a broken and contrite heart.[74] "For we are unto God a sweet savor of Christ, in them that are saved" (2 Corinthians 2:15).

As I've considered the events of this story, I've realized two containers were broken that day: the temporary container of alabaster stone carefully carved by a gifted craftsman and a temporary container of common dust meticulously fashioned by the Master Craftsman. Two fragrances were poured out to God: the aromatic fragrance of the costly ointment sealed in a box of stone and the aromatic fragrance of a priceless love sealed in a heart of stone. As I hold the two in comparison, I must concede there is no contest. The woman's love was the most precious outpouring—the priceless fragrance of a broken and contrite heart is a precious fragrance to God. Then, seeing her wall had fallen and her heart exposed, Jesus sowed these most precious seeds of life: "Thy sins are forgiven…. Thy faith hath saved thee; go in peace" (Luke 7:48, 50).

> But the flesh itself counts for nothing. It's been appointed to die and return to the earth so the spirit within can return to God.

Our true value as God's creation is *not* our temporary containers of flesh—never. Our bodies are just vessels, houses,[75] tabernacles in the wilderness.[76] Our bodies are temporary temples made from dust for birthing, hosting, and developing God's spiritual seed. But the flesh itself counts for nothing. It's been appointed to die and return to the earth so the spirit within can return to God.[77] Our natural bodies will surely die, but those who've been born again through eternal fertilization will rise from the dust to new and glorious heights as a precious fragrance to God—the Father of spirits.[78]

No flesh should glory in his presence.

1 CORINTHIANS 1:29, ITALICS ADDED

The Lord is nigh unto them that are of a broken heart;
and saveth such as be of a contrite spirit.

PSALM 34:18

We have this treasure in earthen vessels, that the excellency of the
power may be of God, and not of us.

2 CORINTHIANS 4:7

Section IV—The Hidden Mystery

But we speak the wisdom of God in a mystery, even the hidden wisdom, which God ordained before the world unto our glory.

1 CORINTHIANS 2:7

10

Treasure Hunters

For where your treasure is, there will your heart be also.

LUKE 12:34

Treasure hunters can certainly excite my fantasy. You can see their workboats lying in harbors throughout the long chain of tropical islands linking North America and South America. Most of these vessels are laden with modern-day equipment for exploring the deep abyss and retrieving hidden bounty. I'd love to board one of those boats with those intrepid men and seek sunken treasures from days gone by. What an adventure!

But facing reality, I don't think it's going to happen. I don't think I'll ever plunge those alluring depths where the stores of lost fortunes and forgotten dreams lie sleeping in Davy Jones's locker.

> I've set my sights on the mystery that's been hidden in God from the beginning of the world—the mystery of fellowship.

I've chosen a more calculated risk and set my sights on something far better—of infinitely greater value—something far more glorious than the illusions of gold or silver. I've set my sights on the mystery that's been hidden in God from the beginning of the world—the mystery of fellowship.]

And to make all men see what is the fellowship [koinōnia: partnership, participation, (social) intercourse, or communion] of *the mystery*, which from the beginning of the world hath been *hid in God*. (Ephesians 3:9, italics added)

Much like treasure lying in the deepest abyss of the ocean, the pearls of wisdom and knowledge submerged in Scripture will remain unexplored and undiscovered until we cease speculation from the surface waters of shallow opinions and boldly plunge into the fathomless depths of its divinely inspired writings.[79] Throughout the Bible, both the Old and New Testament authors claimed to be writing God's inspired word to all of us—Jews, Christians, every nation, every tongue, and every individual on earth, declaring, "For God so loved the world" (John 3:16), "and in his name shall the Gentiles trust" (Matthew 12:21).

> ...searching Scripture has everything to do with treasure hunting in the spiritual realm...

As we explore the depths of God's mystery throughout this work, I hope to help all readers see the incredible longing for fellowship that was hidden in God before he created anything. I also hope to show how the best answer to mankind's universal question about why we were created has everything to do with God making us his treasure and him, ours. So searching Scripture has everything to do with treasure hunting in the spiritual realm, with plunging into the depths of God's heart for this pearl of great value and then paying the price to own it.[80]

And having found *one* pearl of great price, he went and sold all that he had, and bought it. (Matthew 13:46, ASV, italics added)

To get to the bottom of this mystery of God that was foreordained for our glory,[81] we must look to the mission statement Jesus made in his last hours before his crucifixion. On that historic night when Jesus prayed for the success of his mission, he unveiled this mystery in God's heart when he told the world why God had sent him.

Jesus Christ was a man on a mission with a primary objective. Sometimes, however, as in the case of Christ, a mission doesn't originate in the man's own heart but in the heart of the one who sends him.[82] Accordingly, the one who is sent is under the sender's authority to execute his commands and accomplish his purpose, and so it was with Christ. As the first begotten Son of God, Jesus was appointed to unveil the mystery of God and to finish God's work (see Hebrews 3:2).

My meat is to do the will of him that sent me, and *to finish his work*. (John 4:34 italics added)

So what was this mystery? What was this unfinished work that God foreordained for our glory? His mystery wasn't our resurrection. The beautiful promise of a resurrection to everlasting life was known from the beginning, for ages and generations past.[83] Enoch knew about the resurrection and spoke about it when he prophesied to the post-flood generations saying, "Behold, the Lord cometh with ten thousands of his saints" (Jude 1:14). Job knew about the resurrection and prophesied about it saying, "And though after my skin worms destroy this body, yet in my flesh shall I see God" (Job 19:26). Even Mary and Martha were aware of the coming resurrection.[84] But there was a mystery in God's heart that was undisclosed until that Passover night when Jesus prayed for the success of his mission, a mystery that had been hidden in God from before the world was, a mystery that was not manifested to the saints until Christ revealed it to his disciples on the eve of his crucifixion, at God's appointed hour. The glorious mystery that had been hidden in God since before the foundation of the world, was that the nature of Christ would be formed in us to make us one with the Father and the Son.

Even the mystery which hath been hid from ages and from generations, but now is made manifest to his saints: To whom God would make known what is the riches of the glory of this mystery among the Gentiles; which is *Christ in you, the hope of glory.* (Colossians 1:26–27, italics added)

> The glorious mystery that had been hidden in God since before the foundation of the world, was that the nature of Christ would be formed in us to make us one with the Father and the Son.

Our Father told us about the events of the resurrection long before the flood (see Jude 1:14), but he didn't clearly tell us *why* he wanted to resurrect us to an everlasting life with him. This incredible mystery of fellowship in the heart of God wasn't fully revealed until Jesus disclosed it to his closest disciples on the night of the last supper. By looking at the mission statement Jesus made at the Father's appointed hour, we can discover the great treasure that was hidden in God's heart from before the beginning of the world—the pearl of great price.

We are God's treasure, so his heart is for us.

JOHNNY L. DUDLEY

But we have this treasure [the earnest of God's Spirit] in earthen vessels, that the excellency of the power may be of God, and not of us.

2 CORINTHIANS 4:7

Having made known unto us *the mystery of his will,* according to his good pleasure which he hath purposed in himself: That in the dispensation of the fulness of times he might gather together in one all things in Christ, both which are in heaven, and which are on earth; even in him.

EPHESIANS 1:9–10, ITALICS ADDED

And this is *the will of him* [God the Father] that sent me, that everyone which seeth the Son, and believeth on him, may have everlasting life: and I will raise him up at the last day.

JOHN 6:40, ITALICS ADDED

Eye hath not seen, nor ear heard, neither have entered into the heart of man, the things which God hath prepared for them that love him.

1 CORINTHIANS 2:9

Behold, what manner of love the Father hath bestowed upon us, that we should be called *the sons of God.*

1 JOHN 3:1, ITALICS ADDED

11

The Mission Statement 🍃

At that day ye shall know that I am in my Father,
and ye in me, and I in you.

JOHN 14:20

Most of us have heard, read, or written mission statements. They're intended to give the reason for an action by stating the primary objective. We formulate these statements in various ways—some written, some spoken, some are the hidden desires of the heart. They may address our daily affairs, the purpose of a project, or even the direction for our lives or businesses. They are the dreams that define our goals, making us continually aware of our successes and failures. We put our hopes in these dreams and believe, if we can fulfill them, we'll find the priceless treasures of peace and joy.

When we reach the end of our natural lives and are faced with the present reality of death, our dreams will often become more vivid. Against the dark backdrop of death's impending shadow, the hidden issues in our hearts become more clearly defined and more easily stated. For this reason, at our earthly life's postlude we tend to open our souls and pour out the most important matters of our hearts to those we love—and so it was with Christ.

On the eve of his crucifixion, Jesus came face to face with the present reality of his imminent, cruel, and horrific death. The encroaching shadow was no longer a future event. His hour had come,[85] and the weight of the world loomed as the unbearable burden he must bear on a debasing Roman cross. Therefore, immediately after leaving the upper room with his closest disciples and under the horrendous pressure of the impending judgment, Jesus opened his heart and poured out the most cherished secret of his soul, the mystery of fellowship that had been hidden in God from before the beginning of the world, the mystery that we could be one with them, Jesus prayed,

"I do not pray for these alone, but also for those who will believe in Me through their word; that they all may be one, as You, Father, are in Me, and I in You; that they also may be one in Us, that the world may believe You sent Me. And the glory which You gave Me I have given them, that they may be one just as We are one: I in them, and You in Me; that they may be made perfect in one, and that the world may know that You have sent Me, *and have loved them as You have loved me*" (John 17:20–23, NKJV, italics added).

> ...that many would be born of God's Spirit and become one with Christ, so we all could be one with God.

Jesus was one with the Father, so in the cry of his heart was the heart-cry of God—that we, too, may be one with them—God in us, Christ in us, and us in God and us in Christ—joint heirs of God who would be glorified together with Christ.[86] Jesus was born to bear witness to the truth,[87] and that's precisely what he did. In the closing scenes of his earthly mission before he was impaled on the cross, Jesus bore witness to that most beautiful mystery that had been hidden in God's heart from before the beginning, that many would be born of God's Spirit and become one with Christ, so we all could be one with God.

Jesus was foreordained to be our redeemer from before the foundation of the world,[88] and we were predestined to be conformed to his image from before the foundation of the world, so we could be glorified together.[89] This remarkable mystery of fellowship in our Father's heart was all about his eternal longing to make us his priceless treasure and he ours. It was about raising a family: about him loving us with all of his heart and us loving him with all of ours, about God loving man and man loving God with all of their heart, mind, soul, and strength, so they could share in the joys of an everlasting union. How good is that? It's better than gold.

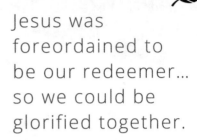

Jesus was foreordained to be our redeemer… so we could be glorified together.

Our omniscient Father longed for intimate relationships of the heart before he created the world[90] and created us for his pleasure.[91] Our Creator God, who declares the end from the beginning,[92] understood that to satisfy his own eternal longing for this highest union of beings, he must create life in his image, according to his likeness,[93] and then make us one with him in the bonds of love. David touched on this miracle of regeneration when he wrote, "Thy word have I hid in mine heart, that I might not sin against thee" (Psalm 119:11).

Our Creator knew that to accomplish this highest of goals with us, we must be spiritually compatible with him. We must be born of his Spirit to share his nature, and we must share his nature to have the strength of heart to faithfully return his love and be one. But as we shall see, cultivating God's divine nature in our hearts is the most challenging part of our development, because it involves our free will.

Creating our natural bodies to be living souls was far less complicated than forming the nature of Christ within us. The natural creation of our bodies precluded our involvement; whereas, cultivating God's divine nature within us entails our wholehearted involvement, and that complicates things immensely. But God had a plan. He always has a plan. His plan was to smelt our hearts in the furnace of the earth until our will was aligned with his and our hearts were made like his.

I and my Father are one.

JOHN 10:30

And I [Jesus] have declared unto them [us] thy name,
and will declare it: *that the love wherewith thou hast loved me
may be in them*, and I in them.

JOHN 17:26, ITALICS ADDED

Holy Father, keep through thine own name those whom thou hast
given me, that they may be one, as we are.

JOHN 17:11, ITALICS ADDED

For I reckon that the sufferings of this present time are not worthy
to be compared with the glory which shall be revealed in us.

ROMANS 8:18

12

Obtain or Become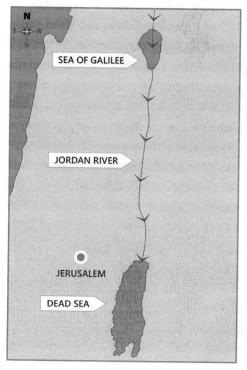

He that believeth on me, as the scripture hath said, out of his
belly shall flow rivers of living water.

JOHN 7:38

My journey to Israel with Mom and her friends made a lasting impression on my life, especially standing on Mount Carmel where Elijah once stood against the prophets of Baal (see 1 Kings 18:17–40). The cool, crisp morning air enhanced my deep awareness of God and filled my cup to the brim with an awesome respect for his holiness.

I'll never forget the morning we spent at the Wailing Wall in Jerusalem, the city of peace that's been steeped in turmoil for millennia. It was so awe-inspiring to be there that I returned alone that afternoon to sit for hours in the midst of the Jewish people and be near them as they prayed, read their scrolls, and stuffed their handwritten petitions into the cracks of the wall. The joints between the large stones were so laden with thousands of heartfelt petitions that there was barely a niche to press any more paper supplications into.

God's presence has overshadowed the wall for many centuries, a feeling that permeated my soul with peace that day.[94] There were many who had come as I had come from around the world, searching for a deeper encounter with God. I didn't want to leave. I felt as if I could have sat there forever. That experience, however, was *not* the highlight of my trip.

Leaving the city of peace, we made our way to the Sea of Galilee to explore the surrounding towns and to boat upon its waters. I was struck by the fertility and abundance of Galilee. The fish markets were filled to feed multitudes with its bounty. I'd never stopped to consider just how rich that inland sea could be. Neither did I realize at the time that my admiration for the profusion of life in Galilee was preparing my heart for the highlight of my trip. In due time, we returned to the bus and headed southward.

The Dead Sea is the lowest place on earth. Its shoreline is reported to be about fourteen hundred feet below sea level, which easily explains why it has no outlet. They say the quantity of water that evaporates from the Dead Sea surpasses the amount of water that flows into it from the Jordan River, giving it one of the highest concentrations of salt in the world. Our guide told us the minerals accumulated in its briny waters are worth billions of dollars. However, even though the Dead Sea is exceedingly abundant in mineral wealth, it cannot support life. It's called the Dead Sea, because it's a hypersaline lake with such a high content of sodium chloride and other mineral salts that it prevents the survival of any aquatic life beyond minuscule quantities of bacteria and fungi.

As we stood beside that dead body of water, our guide knowledgeably shared the sea's history and that of the surrounding area. When he told us the Dead Sea was dead because it had no outlet, my mind became fixed on the spiritual significance of that lifeless, watery desert. The voice of the guide began to fade into the background as an inner voice whispered softly.

> The Dead Sea is wealthy, but it is dead.

I moved away from the crowd, astounded. I had never heard of, nor considered, such an incredible allegory between those two inland seas, the Dead Sea and the Sea of Galilee. The memory of my lesson that day has stayed with me all these years, confronting my soul time and again, especially while on my sojourn through Baca. Years later, I took the time to record that experience, and now I wish to share my experience with you.

One River, Two Seas

From the north it flows, coursing downward through the midst of the holy people, bringing nutrients of life to enrich their thirsty land. The Jordan is a great river, not because of its width, nor its depth, but because it's a river of life. It flows first to the Sea of Galilee where the nutrients are received, increased, and passed on, then to the Dead Sea where the nutrients are only received.

> Could it be, God reveals the secret of life in the geography of this holy land?

The Sea of Galilee receives from the north and passes its blessing on, while the Dead Sea receives from the north and hoards the life-giving nutrients. The Sea of Galilee is one with the river and shares in the joys of life, while the Dead Sea just obtains what the river gives and swallows the blessing, bringing an unfruitful end to the life-giving flow. Like its progenitor, the Sea of Galilee has become a life giver, but to the contrary, the Dead Sea has merely obtained the benefits of the river and has become a consumer, a repository of lifeless wealth. Galilee teems with life and gives life again. The Dead Sea is wealthy, but it is dead.

From the shores of its lifeless waters, I stood and gazed across the vast mineral stores of the Dead Sea's immense wealth and onward to the north from where the Jordan flows. My eyes turned from the desolate valley of salt toward the source of the teeming river, and I pondered the mystery of the two seas—both recipients of the Jordan's life-giving flow. Could it be, God reveals the secret of life in the geography of this holy land?

Both receive God's life, but only one receives his nature.

In my understanding, the two seas revealed the two most basic differences in man's response to God the Life Giver—either obtain or become. Every living soul is born of the River of Life that proceeds from the heart of God. However, like the two seas, the outcome of their choices can be drastically different— either life or death. Like the Sea of Galilee, one will receive the life-giving flow of God's love, reaching, embracing, and reproducing his divine characteristics, then becoming one with the source and passing it on with unbroken continuity. Yet like the Dead Sea, another will receive God's life-giving flow and merely obtain his blessings, selfishly hoard them, and then continue to degenerate through increasing self-absorption. The former becomes one with God and lives, but the latter merely obtains what God has created and dies. Both receive God's life, but only one receives his nature.

Our omniscient Creator, who knows and declares the end from the beginning, knew and understood this great secret of life before he began his acts of creation. He knew it was greater to give than to receive, that the heart finds life when the nutrients of love flow outward, toward others, from deep within us.

When love flows from the holiest place of our souls, life is increased and passed on in a continuous flow of God's creative expression. It must flow outward with such a life-giving passion and power that it surpasses the fear of dying to self so that in the likeness of Christ, we would lay down our lives before we would violate the precepts of love. As with the Sea of Galilee, we must become givers of life to share in the joy of life with the life giver—with God—"the fountain of living waters" (Jeremiah 17:13).

God also knew and understood the enemy of life before implementing his acts of creation. He knew our greatest threat as the heirs of his glory would be becoming self-absorbed. When our love becomes self-directed, it becomes isolated and stagnant, unbalanced, a hypersaline pool of perilous thought that compels us to obtain all we can,[95] even unto the shedding of another's blood. As with the Dead Sea, we may gain vast deposits of valuable and intellectual treasures, but if we withhold our love, we will stagnate within and die, because life self-destructs when love self-directs.

There is a river whose streams make glad the people of God. It flows from the sides of the north, from the mount of the congregation,[96] from the throne of God and of the Lamb.[97] As it flows, it courses down through the hearts of the holy people bringing the nutrients of life to enrich their thirsty souls. It is a great river, not because of its width nor its depth, but because it is a river of life. It flows clear as crystal from Zion's holy hill,[98] and the source of that great river is the wellspring of love flowing from the Father's heart.

Just as the Sea of Galilee receives from the north and becomes one with its source, we must receive from the north (see Psalm 48:2) and become one with our source. We must receive, increase, and pass on the life-giving nutrients of that holy river that tirelessly flows from the heart of God. We must pass it on with unbroken continuity, without fear, reservation, or selfish motives. God is the giver of life, so for us to become one with the Life Giver, we must become life givers as well, tributaries to his great river, partakers of the divine nature.

It's more blessed to give than to receive.

ACTS 20:35

He that believeth on me, as the scripture hath said,
out of his belly shall flow rivers of living water.

JOHN 7:38

For my people have committed two evils; they have forsaken me
the fountain of living waters, and hewed them out cisterns,
broken cisterns, that can hold no water.

JEREMIAH 2:13

Section V—The Spiritual Connection

Life self-destructs when love self-directs.

JOHNNY L. DUDLEY

13

The Cycle of Life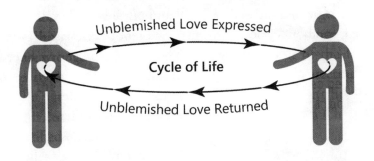

He that loveth not knoweth not God; for God is love.

1 JOHN 4:8

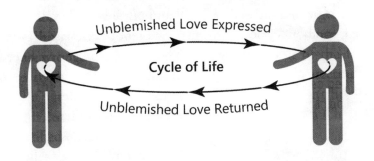

Unblemished Love Expressed

Cycle of Life

Unblemished Love Returned

B eing loved is easy, requiring little to no effort at all. I've been loved all my life by family, friends, and, according to the Holy Scriptures, even God. Returning love is where the work starts. Whether it's to God or others, returning love is where the high price for love is paid.

This truth impacted me early one December morning as I labored with deep and agonizing remorse, pleading for God to take my weakness from me and set me free. Years of self-indulgence had yielded more bitter fruits and painful regrets than I cared to remember. I don't know how many times through those years I had appealed to God to take my indiscretions from me, but it wasn't until that early winter morning, in the darkest hours before the dawn, when I heard his subtle whisper speak to my heart and say, "I will not take it; I want you to give it. Love must be freely given to satisfy the heart."

> ...returning love is where the high price for love is paid.

Love is not a shotgun wedding. God will not invade our hearts and force us to return his love. Forcing one's will upon another is contrary to the ways of love. Love must be freely given and freely returned to satisfy the heart with the joy of true communion. Many of us have learned this through years of experience and have found it confirmed in the counsel of God's word. Love must be freely exchanged to know the highest blessing of life. It must be expressed and then returned as a holy sacrifice from both hearts before our walls will fall and our love will cycle.

Life is all about cycles. In the first chapter of Ecclesiastes, Solomon brings our attention to how the whole realm of creation revolves

> "I will not take it; I want you to give it. Love must be freely given to satisfy the heart."

around cycles—the cycle of a man's labors, cycles of the sun, cycles of the wind, and the cycles of the rivers. Cycles are necessary for our environment's health, as well as our physical and emotional health.

Who would want to live forever without the joy of love in full cycle? Jesus endured the cross to bear our sins and return God's love as our forerunner, so he could obtain the joy that was set before him.[99] Therefore, joy is key, the joy of love in full cycle between the Father and us is the substance of our great salvation. When Jesus went to the cross to obtain this joy, he set the example for us to follow. Through his faithful performance of love at Calvary and beyond, Jesus showed us the narrow way that leads to life is all about returning God's love with the same standard he gives it. This spiritual cycle between God and man began with God's love being expressed toward men and was made perfect when his love was freely returned by a man—Christ Jesus.

For there is one God, and one mediator between God and men, the man Christ Jesus. (1 Timothy 2:5)

When love cycles from heart to heart under these rewarding conditions, it makes life timeless and fulfilling, worth living forever. It empowers the greatest cycle of all—the cycle of life. You won't find the term *cycle of life* written in the pages of Scripture, but you will see it pursued from the first verse of Genesis to the cross of Calvary and forward to the last sentence in Revelation. Expressing love from the heart

Love must be freely exchanged to know the highest blessing of life.

is how God began this life-giving cycle with us, and his love will have accomplished its most perfect work when we return our love to him—in like manner—freely from the heart.

Our omniscient Father, who declares the end from the beginning, loved us before he created us. He chose to create us in Christ Jesus from before the foundation of the world (see Ephesians 2:10), so we could be holy and without blame before him in love (see Ephesians 1:4). Our Creator God and Father planned for us to partner with him in this spiritual exchange as mirrored reflections of his love so we could be one in heart, mind, soul, and strength. Then he sent his only begotten Son to demonstrate this great love for us (see John 3:16, NKJV), so we could learn how to follow his Son and return his standard of love. The more I think about God sending his firstborn into the violence of this world to initiate this cycle between us, the more I realize just how much our Father truly loves us and longs to be one spirit with us.

But he that is joined unto the Lord is one spirit. (1 Corinthians 6:17)

According to Jesus's prayer on the night preceding his passion, it is God in us and us in God that completes this life-giving cycle.[100] But how do we do this? How do we follow our forerunner into that holiest place of God to return his love and perfect the cycle?

The good news is, the answer is presented in Scripture. It's given to us through a simple set of instructions called *the pattern*, which we are going to explore throughout the remainder of this book. The pattern is God's clear and pointed instructions for returning his love and becoming one in heart, mind, soul, and strength.

> As branches, we receive God's life by abiding in Christ, the vine, because Christ abides in God, the source.

God's pattern charts our course to the holiest place of God, which is why the Levites used it for building the tabernacle in the wilderness. It provided the Levite priests with divine instructions for entering God's holiest place to atone for the sins of the people and the instructions Jesus followed to atone for the sins of the world. And as we shall see in the coming chapters, they are the instructions we must use to follow Christ.

Abiding in the Vine

On the eve of his crucifixion, Jesus said many important things to the world by telling those things to his disciples. Among them was the analogy he gave about his intended relationship with us, saying, "I am the vine; ye are the branches: He that abideth in me, and I in him, the same bringeth forth much fruit: for without me ye can do nothing" (John 15:5).

> God is love, and true love demands expression.

In this scriptural analogy of Christ, the vine, and ourselves, the branches, Jesus taught us that a fruit-bearing relationship with God is based entirely on this life-giving cycle.

As branches, we receive God's life by abiding in Christ, the vine, because Christ abides in God, the source. But this analogy goes deeper, for the branch not only receives its life from the vine, but it also gives life back to the vine. In the natural world, we call this process photosynthesis. Both the vine and the branch must give of themselves to complete the life-giving cycle and bear a perfect fruit to the husbandman of the vineyard. If not, the branch will either be purged or taken away. Jesus said, "I am the true vine, and my Father is the husbandman.

> Expression was called "The Word of God.

Every branch in me that beareth not fruit he taketh away: and every branch that beareth fruit, he purgeth it, that it may bring forth more fruit" (John 15:1–2).

Love began its circular exchange in the heart of God, because God is love, and true love demands expression. The great love of God would not be contained in eternal isolation, so God released his expression and commenced his creation. Expression was called "The Word of God" (Revelation 19:13).

In the beginning was the Word, and the Word was with God, and the Word was God. (John 1:1)

From the holiest place in the heart of God, love began its flow as an endless river of life, initiating and sustaining his progenitive acts through the power and authority of the Word.[101] Our omniscient Father released the only power great enough to initiate, convey, and sustain eternal life with the steadfast constant of joy—his love expressed. For where there is love, pure love, eternal and undefiled, there will also be eternal life.

God is love.

1 JOHN 4:8

According as he hath chosen us in him before the foundation of the world, that we should be holy and without blame before him in love

EPHESIANS 1:4

**I am the Alpha and Omega, the First and the Last,
the Beginning [God's love expressed] *and the End* [God's love returned].**

REVELATION 22:13, ITALICS ADDED

So shall my word be that goeth forth out of my mouth: it shall not return unto me void, but it shall accomplish that which I please, and it shall prosper in the thing whereto I sent it.

ISAIAH 55:11

14

The Secret Place 🌿

He who dwells in the secret place of the Most High shall abide
under the shadow of the Almighty.

PSALM 91:1, NKJV

have often pondered the secret place of the Most High. I firmly
believe that to be intimately acquainted with God's Spirit in this
most secret place of his soul is the greatest blessing a conscious
mind could attempt to conceive. This mysterious place in the heart
of God is the most intimate place of his soul—his holiest place. It's
where his Spirit dwells, harboring
his most secret thoughts and his
deepest emotions.

> ...it's the holiest place
> of the soul where
> our consciousness
> dwells.

God has a soul,[102] and his
soul has a secret place. In fact,
every living soul made in God's
image has a secret place like his
where we harbor our most secret
thoughts and deepest emotions. Scripture calls it the heart, or the
inner man,[103] because it's the holiest place of the soul where our
consciousness dwells. In this most sacred place of the living soul, our
spirits can meld with God's and God's with ours to become one in

heart, mind, soul, and strength—to know him as we are known (see 1 Corinthians 13:12).

We were designed to be one with God and others through a flawless union of spirits. This is why the Scripture declares, "He that is joined unto the Lord is one spirit" (1 Corinthians 6:17), and again, we "are builded together for the habitation of God through the Spirit" (Ephesians 2:22). God can enter this holiest place of our hearts to inhabit us by his Spirit, and we can enter this holiest place of his heart, to inhabit him by our spirit; that is, if we've been born again of his Spirit.[104] If God's Spirit is born within us through the regenerative process of eternal fertilization, the author of Hebrews says we can have the boldness to enter into God's holiest place by the blood of Jesus (see Hebrews 10:19). Paul also confirmed this when he wrote to the Ephesian church and said, "For through him [Christ Jesus] we both have access by one Spirit unto the Father" (2:18).

We were made to know our Father as intimately as we know ourselves, to know his Spirit in the holiest place of his soul and for him to know our spirits in the holiest place of ours.[105] This is the way life cycles between the Father and the Son, so it's the way it must cycle between the Father and us to make us one with them—joint heirs of God's glory. Jesus defined this intimate spiritual connection as *God in us and us in God* (see John 17:21).

Looking back to that most notable Passover night, Jesus passionately prayed that all who believed in him would become one with him and his Father in this life-giving cycle of spirits.[106] His prayer was about God in us and us in God through the intimate union of unblemished spirits. He was talking about a chosen people, a brotherhood, a royal priesthood,[107] a family of men and women who would be one with the Father and with the Son through the only life-giving force that wields the power of an endless life—the Holy Spirit. But to make this holy connection with God and others our supreme reality, it would help to understand how the living soul works.

We are going to begin exploring God's spiritual instructions for approaching and entering his holiest place in the coming chapters; but for now, I'd like to remain focused on what it is.

Again, the secret place of the living soul is the holiest place of the soul—the heart. It's the seat of our conscious awareness where we implant, embrace, and nurture the many seeds of thought that form our indelible nature. This most private chamber of the living soul is where our spirit dwells and where our spiritual connections are made to make us one. Anyone accepted in this most private place of another's soul will have the power to hold that person's heart in their hands, so faithfulness is mandatory, it's the rock we build on. Therefore, if the threat of being violated or hurt is discerned in the heart of either person in the spiritual connection, an emotional wall will rise between us and stop the spiritual cycle. And as we shall continue to see, the human heart does not sit still; it is either building bridges or building walls.

> This most private chamber of the living soul is where our spirit dwells and where our spiritual connections are made to make us one.

> ...the human heart does not sit still; it is either building bridges or building walls.

Scripture gives a clear record that before the events of Calvary, God protected this secret place of his heart with an emotional wall like ours. His veil was a curtained wall or barrier that kept all men on the outside of this holiest place until the appointed time when they could be sanctified for the union—until they could be cleansed by the blood of God's Lamb and born again of his Spirit.

Our walls do the same thing. They don't allow anyone to enter without clean hands and pure hearts, because these walls were designed to protect our hearts from emotional violations by unfaithful people. In the likeness of our Creator God who created us in his image, we are able to choose who we will keep on the outside of our walls or who we will accept beyond our walls for an intimate spiritual connection.

In the gospel of Matthew, Jesus told us many are called but few are chosen (see 22:14), which means God exercises this freedom of choice toward us individually, and he has a criterion for his choices. Therefore, it would seem wise for us to learn how to follow his pattern's instructions for acceptance beyond his veil.

> The pattern has shown the world how to be accepted in God's holiest place.

The pattern God gave Moses on Mount Sinai showed us the proper protocol for entering into the holiest place of God to commune with his Spirit.[108] This is why the pattern was the blueprint for building the tabernacle in the wilderness. It has shown the world how to be accepted in God's holiest place. And as we shall see, God's pattern also shows us how to be accepted in the hearts of every living soul he's made in his image.

But there's more. As a figure of the true tabernacle in the heavens, the tabernacle in the wilderness showed us how Christ, after becoming the sins of our world, would be accepted in God's holiest place for his reconciliation and ours. Therefore, to understand how the pattern works is to understand how to follow Christ, and to understand how to follow Christ is to understand how to be accepted in God's holiest place.

The pattern shows us how to be reconciled with God and establish an intimate spiritual connection with him, no matter how unclean we've become, by putting our faith in Christ for our cleansing and following its simple instructions. It charts our course through the narrow way that leads to life with God and others, which is why it can take us from the lowest point in Baca's valley to the highest place in the heart of God regardless of our past.

For Christ is not entered into the holy places made with hands, *which are the figures of the true*; but into heaven itself, now to appear in the presence of God for us. (Hebrews 9:24, italics added)

...the pattern has everything to do with removing walls and building bridges.

From the creation of the first Adam until the crucifixion of the last, the natural man could only walk in phileo love with God.[109] No man, including Enoch, Noah, Abraham, or David could consistently return God's righteous standard of love to be accepted as one in his holiest place, that is, until our righteous forerunner met the pattern's requirements for our cleansing and brought us nigh by the blood of his sacrifice. So the pattern has everything to do with removing walls and building bridges.

Understanding the utility of God's pattern for building spiritual bridges is essential for understanding the heart and soul of Scripture, and the heart and soul of this book. But to truly understand how God's pattern works, we need to thoroughly understand that *God's veil is the focal point of the pattern* and *removing his veil is the function of the pattern*.

And the veil of the temple was rent in twain from the top to the bottom. (Mark 15:38)

But now in Christ Jesus ye who sometimes were far off
are *made nigh by the blood of Christ.*

EPHESIANS 2:13, ITALICS ADDED

Having therefore, brethren, *boldness to enter into the holiest*
by the blood of Jesus.

HEBREWS 10:19, ITALICS ADDED

For he hath made him to be sin for us, who knew no sin;
that we might be made the righteousness of God in him.

2 CORINTHIANS 5:21

15

The Wall 🍃

The veil shall be a divider for you between
the holy place and the Most Holy.

EXODUS 26:33, NKJV

There was a wall between us. The unfaithful actions of my long-time friend and business partner had triggered an emotional barrier deep down in my soul, and it seemed there was nothing I could do to remove it. Although things had started well, in due time our relationship was seriously damaged and an emotional wall came between us.

When any person threatens to violate our physical, financial, or emotional health or security, a wall crops up inside of us. No one can see the wall because it's not tangible, but it's there all the same, and people can discern it in their spirit. The cause of the wall's presence might be more of a deep reaction in the soul than a decision of the mind, yet the mind is certainly involved. When relational

> No one can see the wall because it's not tangible, but it's there all the same, and people can discern it in their spirit.

violations are committed without regard for our well-being, the wall is immediately triggered.

Through the many years of shared adventures, I'd observed some flaws in his character, especially when it came to money, but I had seen flaws in my character too, so I tried to be patient with his. I suppose I believed he'd be faithful to me in business because of our friendship. Perhaps his problem was too deeply rooted in his nature; I'm not even sure he tried to control it. If you give a chocoholic access to a chocolate shop, you could expect the temptation would overwhelm them sooner or later. Perhaps I was just naïve.

I was deeply invested in his business and the pressure was building. The question constantly on the table was, did I throw more good money after the bad? The business's potential was incredible, but the excessive costs were soaring out of control, way beyond my initial commitment. I wanted my friend to be successful and hoped for a good return on my investment, so I reluctantly continued my support. There were several years of ongoing cash calls until I caught his hand in the cookie jar.

My friend's first problem was he couldn't be trusted with other people's money. His greater problem was *he justified his actions in his heart*. When I became aware of some things he had done, I was hurt and the wall went up inside of me. I didn't want the wall between us, he'd been my friend and comrade for years, but I couldn't remove it even though I really wanted it to go away. He tried to continue our relationship as though nothing had happened, but that didn't work too well for me because he never even attempted restitution. I felt like he'd shown his hand and *I wasn't in it*, so the wall remained.

I've learned some painful lessons on both sides of these emotional walls as the violator and the violated, but my painful lessons have produced some very redeeming benefits. They helped me to understand the function of the veil before the holiest place of God's heart, and why it had to remain intact until Christ gave God the confidence to remove it by fulfilling the law of love for us.

The veil is taken away in Christ. (2 Corinthians 3:14)

God's Wall

And after the second veil, the tabernacle which is called the
Holiest of all. (Hebrews 9:3)

Looking back to the first Adam, it's easy to see why God kept
him at a distance. If God had allowed Adam to go beyond the veil
and enter his holiest place without the nature of Christ being formed
within him,[110] God's Spirit would've been joined to a callow man with
a self-serving nature. It would have been a recipe for disaster. So God
didn't let Adam in. Our heavenly Father maintained his veil until his
conditions for entry were met through Christ, who as our forerunner
[111] was a minister of the true tabernacle in the heavens and the first
Son of man to be accepted beyond God's veil.[112]

Our forefather Adam was purely human, which explains why he
could never have been the forerunner of man into that secret place
of God to be one with his spirit. He was corruptible and wasn't
trustworthy. Therefore, Adam couldn't be trusted to love God with
all his heart and that's what justified God's veil. His veil would remain
intact until Jesus, the forerunner and advocate of man, would meet
the pattern's requirements for removing God's veil and making our
connection possible.

Having therefore, brethren, boldness to enter into the holiest by
the blood of Jesus. (Hebrews 10:19)

Again, the veil is what the heavenly pattern is all about—it's the
focal point of the pattern. Everything about the pattern has to do with
removing the veil for spiritual communion. It begins with cleansing
our hearts through restitution and then preparing our hearts through
spiritual renewal. Therefore, taking up our cross and following Christ
through every step in the pattern pertains to our own sanctification
for spiritual communion—for acceptance in God's beloved.

To the praise of the glory of his grace, wherein he hath made us accepted in the beloved. (Ephesians 1:6)

So the pattern shows us several important things about how the living soul works—our walls are designed to protect our hearts, and removing our walls is necessary for building bridges. It shows us that true reconciliation with God or man requires more than just sacrifice, it also requires a change of heart. This is one of the reasons why animal sacrifices could never remove God's veil or consummate his spiritual connection with us. They stayed the laws demand for our eternal judgment, but they didn't change our hearts. They were merely "a shadow of good things to come" (Hebrews 10:1).

How could animal sacrifices give God the assurance that any man's heart was faithful, true, and trustworthy? They couldn't and they didn't. Sacrificing an animal's life for our restitution is not even close to faithfulness that's required for yielding our will and renewing the right spirit within us. The sacrifice of animals covered our immediate transgressions and postponed our eternal judgment (see Revelation 20:13), but they couldn't cleanse our hearts or change our nature from the carnal to the divine. But the one sacrifice for sin Jesus made was different. He took our sins to the grave and imputed his righteousness to us, so we could follow him to God's mercy seat with a cleansed and renewed heart to complete our role in the ministry of reconciliation with God.

> They stayed the laws demand for our eternal judgment, but they didn't change our hearts.

And there I will meet with thee, and I will commune with thee from above the mercy seat. (Exodus 25:22)

Adam was created to commune with God, to drink living waters from the fountain of life in the heart of God, but Adam wasn't quite ready to drink those living waters because his spirit was not yet compatible with God's Spirit. So I am willing to bet that Adam was among the first to eagerly receive God's spiritual seed when Jesus preached for deliverance of those spirits who lived before the flood.[113]

> So I am willing to bet that Adam was among the first to eagerly receive God's spiritual seed when Jesus preached for deliverance of those spirits who lived before the flood.

Surely, Adam's longing to be restored to the face of God burned in his heart from the day of his fall, and surely God's longing to be restored to the face of Adam burned in his heart too. I believe they both felt the pain and sorrow of broken trust and longed for reconciliation. But just like the rest of us, Adam needed to be born again of God's Spirit before he could soar the high and lofty places of the One who inhabits eternity. Adam was a caterpillar, not a butterfly.[114]

> Adam was a caterpillar, not a butterfly.

Receive with meekness the engrafted word,
which is able to save your souls.

JAMES 1:21

My little children, of whom I travail in birth again
until Christ be formed in you.

GALATIANS 4:19

Marvel not that I said unto thee, Ye must be born again.

JOHN 3:7

For with thee is the fountain of life.

PSALM 36:9

16

The Ministry of Reconciliation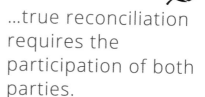

All things are of God, who hath reconciled us to himself by Jesus Christ, and hath given to us the ministry of reconciliation.

2 CORINTHIANS 5:18, ITALICS ADDED

Nobody likes emotional walls, how could we? We were created for intimate spiritual connections to become one with the One who is love (see 1 John 4:8). So both God the Creator and man the created have longed for this higher level of spiritual unity that will no longer be subject to human failure. Because of this, when Paul told the Corinthian church that we have a role in our reconciliation with God, he was spotlighting a commonly held truth that pertains to this longing, which is, true reconciliation requires the participation of both parties.

> ...true reconciliation requires the participation of both parties.

Both persons must do their part to create or recreate harmony in a relationship. In the act of reconciliation, one usually makes restitution and the other forgives. In the case of our reconciliation with God, God has taken the initiative to do both. He has sent his Son to make restitution for us so he could completely forgive us.

God has covered both ends of our breach to ensure our success by making restitution for us through Christ and then forgiving those who accept his restitution. Therefore, our God-given role in this ministry is to respond to God's outreach by putting our faith in the blood of his Son's atoning sacrifice to cleanse us, receive his implanted word for our spiritual transformation, and then follow his Son through the pattern God gave for returning his love. This is how we attain the highest level of life and love that is no longer subject to human failings.

> ...our God-given role in this ministry is to respond to God's outreach by putting our faith in the blood of his Son's atoning sacrifice to cleanse us, receive his implanted word for our spiritual transformation, and then follow his Son through the pattern God gave for returning his love.

Our reconciliation with God is made possible by the works of God to prepare our way and the works of man to return his love. Our reconciliation with God is not a one-way street. We still have a continuing responsibility to accept what he's done and follow his Son with faith in his blood for our cleansing.[115] James bore witness to this responsibility when he said, "Faith without works is dead" (2:20).

In this progressive order of events that began with God's outreach to us and ends with our response to him, we can hear an echo of Jesus's words from the gospel of Matthew, "He that taketh not his cross, and followeth after me, is not worthy of me" (10:38), and

> Our reconciliation with God is not a one-way street.

then again in Luke, "Whosoever doth not bear his cross, and come after me, cannot be my disciple" (14:27). Paul also spoke about our responsibility in this ministry when he said, "*Be ye reconciled to God*" (2 Corinthians 5:20, italics added). Paul's written command to the Corinthian church was addressing everyone's need to complete their role in the ministry of reconciliation with God.

Reconciliation is always a two-way street.

Reconciliation is always a two-way street. But likely in the practice of life, we'll soon discover that our responsibility to participate in this ministry will go hard against the will of our flesh, just as it went against the will of Jesus's flesh in Gethsemane. Jesus asked his Father to take the cup from him *if it were possible* because it went so hard against his will,[116] yet Jesus was faithful to yield his will and commit himself to the Father saying, "Not my will, but thine, be done." This faithfulness is what sets Jesus apart.

Yielding our will is an act of personal sacrifice that always costs something—it's the way Jesus went to reconcile us to God and the way we must go to follow him. True to my carnal nature, I've learned these things the hard way as told below.

The Offense

We were close, very close, and we shared a lot of great memories together. In time, however, I committed a serious offense that shattered her confidence in my faithfulness and made her afraid to trust me. Her hurt gave rise to a wall between us that couldn't be penetrated, bypassed, or removed at will, even though we both wanted it to go away. So even though we still loved each other from the heart, trust had been violated and the life-giving flow couldn't cycle. How could love cycle? Her emotional wall had blocked our spiritual connection and our joy had died immediately. So before she could remove her wall and expose her heart to mine again, the onus was on me to make the kind of restitution that would restore her confidence in me and reconcile our hearts. But where did I start?

To rebuild and maintain such a priceless connection is not so easily done by a natural man with a carnal mind and a corruptible heart. Adam certainly couldn't do it in Eden. He was intelligent enough to want that priceless connection with God and Eve but not strong enough to build and maintain his end. So for a natural man like me who was first born with the carnal nature of my forefather Adam, the huge question that begged an answer was, how could I fix what I had done? How could I give her the confidence she needed to remove her wall and reestablish a trustworthy connection? The answer is found in the melody of Scripture.

What could be more challenging than for a man who had become the sins of our world to be accepted in the holiest place of God beyond his veil?

I began to examine how Jesus reconciled himself to God after shouldering the sins of our world, which led me to ponder a thought-provoking question: What could be more challenging than for a man who had become the sins of our world to be accepted in the holiest place of God beyond his veil?

By shouldering our sins, Jesus the Christ, the one who had literally shared God's glory before the world was,[117] became so polluted with our sins that he had to be forsaken by God as utterly unacceptable.[118] Once Jesus took the weight of the world on his own shoulders,[119] he became the sin of every human being who had ever lived or ever would live on this planet. Therefore, to reconcile his heart and ours with God's, Jesus had to take the right steps. He had to follow the pattern's instructions for making restitution and renewing the right Spirit within him, so God could remove his veil to receive his firstborn and all of those who would follow him.

Once I realized what Jesus had done and how he had done it, I began to realize that I needed to follow the same steps he took to reconcile my heart with hers, and hers with mine. Jesus, *the most violated man in the history of sin*, was reconciled to God, exalted to God's right hand, and then called faithful and true, simply because he met the pattern's radical requirements for total reconciliation.

It's a true statement that the wall was hers and only she could remove it, but it's also true that the violation was mine and only I could repair it. So again, once I understood what Jesus did to reconcile his heart with God's, I understood what I must do to reconcile my heart with hers.

Looking back to Eden, I can see why the first Adam couldn't connect his heart with God's on the highest plain of spiritual unity. He didn't know faithfulness was mandatory and is the underlying bedrock for building spiritual bridges, or at least he didn't act on it, but neither did I.

As a natural man with a carnal mind, I hadn't understood that my faithfulness to protect her heart from hurt *was necessary for protecting mine*. The painful experience taught me that *faithfulness protects* the joy in both hearts and that *unfaithfulness destroys* the joy in both hearts. I realized I had traded the joy of a lifelong communion with her for the flash of a moment's pleasure.

So foolish was I. (Psalm 73:3)

It's a true statement that the wall was hers and only she could remove it, but it's also true that the violation was mine and only I could repair it.

The Good News

Being justified freely by his grace through the redemption that is in Christ Jesus. (Romans 3:24)

> ...our omniscient Father's plan was to make us one, take us through the valley of Baca, and teach us the importance of love, so he could bring us out of the valley with a faithfulness to love equal to the faithfulness of his firstborn.

The good news of the gospel is, God had plans to build a trustworthy connection from his heart to ours from before the beginning—a spiritual span of heartfelt trust from his heart to ours that would cast out fear, remove all doubt, and break down the wall between us. He had plans to build a bridge on the strength of his Son's faithfulness, so we could follow his lead across the spiritual connection he would build to perfect our joy in the cycle of life.

From before the foundation of the world, our omniscient Father's plan was to make us one, take us through the valley of Baca, and teach us the importance of love, so he could bring us out of the valley with a faithfulness to love equal to the faithfulness of his firstborn. His objective being, we would return his love through our own free will and abolish those oppressive consequences of human failures.

Be ye reconciled to God.

2 CORINTHIANS 5:20

Be reconciled to thy brother.

MATTHEW 5:24

Section VI—A Blueprint for the Bridge

According as his divine power hath given unto us *all things that pertain unto life and godliness.*

2 PETER 1:3, ITALICS ADDED

17

Clear and Pointed Instructions 🍃

Take fast hold of instruction; let *her* not go: keep her;
for she *is* thy life.

PROVERBS 4:13, ITALICS ADDED

God has established laws to govern our universe and everything in it. Laws give us clear and pointed instructions about how things work and how we are supposed to live. Through his laws, our heavenly Father has even instructed us in the rules of conduct for perfecting the joy of unity. By his divine power, God has given us everything that pertains to life and godliness, and this, of course, would include his clear and pointed instructions for building spiritual bridges. But the problem for many of us is, we don't want to be bothered with instructions.

When I think about the need we all have to follow instructions, I'm painfully reminded of the time I bought my first videocassette recorder. VCRs were very costly when they first came out, so the huge investment from my limited finances tainted my excitement with feelings of guilt. The guilt didn't last too long though, because it quickly turned into extreme frustration when I couldn't make my blankety-blank VCR work.

And then, to make matters worse, my wife did the most unspeakable thing. She read the instructions, rearranged the wires, and made it operate the way it was supposed to. Deep down I resented her for that. So I watched our first movie in a conspiracy of silence with humiliated indignation. That was just my first unwanted lesson from our new and overpriced VCR.

I accomplished very little the following day at work. My mind was trained on the approaching evening of a movie blitzkrieg. My investment had already damaged my wallet, so I spent my lunch money renting a tall stack of blockbuster movies.

Coming home as early as I could, I crammed down dinner and prepared myself for an immediate assault on the first movie. I figured doing the dishes was her problem, not mine, so my flimsy excuse for not helping because of much-needed rest added the guilt of lying to the guilt of financial indulgence. It's downright awkward to start a movie when your wife is doing the dishes—alone—and it will never secure an award-winning romance.

To my extreme frustration, the first video I chose from the stack didn't work. After several irritating attempts, I inserted another. None of the videos worked, not one, so it had to be the machine. I suppose I could have referred to the troubleshooting section in the instructions, but that's not my style. I chose the only resolution my already bruised male ego could muster and called the retailer.

After lambasting the salesman and slamming down the phone, I boxed the source of my frustration and headed back to McDuff's appliance store. I could tell they expected me when I stormed through the door, because not one of them said a thing as I smacked the box on the top of the counter. The humble response of the store manager didn't help matters at all—I think I went there expecting a fight. After all, it was their fault. I'd been seriously inconvenienced, and somebody needed to pay.

"Let's take a look," was all he said to defuse my condescending outrage. Opening the door to the video port, he softly announced, "Here's your problem, Mr. Dudley."

The shocking sight of the granola bar and cheese toast my young son had inserted into the port covered the nearby salesmen in a smirk of blanketed silence. I'm quite sure, however, there was a titanic outburst of laughter at my expense when I walked out the door with my hat in my hands.

If pride comes before a fall, then so, too, does the male ego. In my defense, however, we (the males of our species) can't help the embarrassing fact that most of us are born with very little patience and only a pretense of honor, so I sort of lean toward Adam's defense—*it's not really my fault.*

I'm quite convinced my inherent resistance to reading instructions is a predominantly male characteristic, because my son hadn't referred to the instructions either. I do concede he might have read them if he'd been old enough to read, but I have serious doubts.

Similarly, when Peter wrote that our heavenly Father has provided all things pertaining to life and godliness,[120] this would certainly include his spiritual instructions for following Christ and getting our wiring right. If we seek to learn, understand, and follow his spiritual instructions, we will be able to make informed choices that keep us on the right path for the greatest blessing of life—the joy of unity. But if you're a victim of those impatient male genes that despise instructions, please don't discard this book or write to me with a complaint, and please don't mail it back expecting a refund. You must learn to listen to your wife and follow the divine instructions in the manufacturer's handbook called *the Bible*, so you can finish your course with joy.[121]

We will be studying God's pattern for building and sustaining spiritual bridges in the remainder of this book and what our forerunner has done to walk us through it. But I must forewarn you, our Creator's instructions have a narrow focus on life and godliness that may challenge your code of conduct.

For us to follow God's instructions with faith is worth every challenging step. It will transform our souls from mortal beings with carnal minds to immortal beings with spiritual minds—the mind of Christ.[122] But again, there is one huge caveat we must be aware of before we plot our course through the steps of the pattern—we will traverse straight through the heart of Baca on that well-worn path called the Via Dolorosa—the way of the cross.

Looking unto Jesus the author and finisher of our faith; who for the joy that was set before him endured the cross.

HEBREWS 12:2

Then said Jesus unto his disciples, If any man will come after me, let him deny himself, and take up his cross, and follow me.

MATTHEW 16:24

The law of the Lord is perfect, converting the soul.

PSALM 19:7

18

The Law of Love 🌿

For all the law is fulfilled in one word, even in this;
Thou shalt love thy neighbour as thyself.

GALATIANS 5:14

Our omniscient Creator was not ignorant of our weakness before he created our forefather Adam, nor was he unprepared to build his strength within us. He laid the groundwork for strengthening our hearts when he breathed his fundamental laws for life and godliness into Adam's soul, and the human conscience has borne witness to right and wrong ever since.[123] But as stated before, if our forefather's creation had been finished in Eden, the divine nature would've already been formed within him and there never would've been a need for the veil before the secret place of God's heart or for the Lamb to be slain for our transgressions. But God hadn't finished his workmanship in Eden, so the veil was there until it was done away in Christ. The veil had to be there, because our carnal nature would be there until we were created in Christ Jesus, until the Lamb was sent to prepare us for the good works that God had ordained for us to walk in.

For we are his workmanship, *created in Christ Jesus* unto good works, which God hath before ordained that we should walk in them. (Ephesians 2:10, italics added)

Before creation, our omniscient Creator knew the man from Eden would lack two essential elements for the good works of walking in love: a clear *understanding* of the law of love and the *strength* of heart to uphold what he did know. Therefore, when the timing was right, God provided us with the spiritual instructions we needed to strengthen our inner man so we could finish our course with joy—the two fatherly dictates from Mount Sinai—the Ten Commandments and the heavenly pattern.

> The letter of the law governs our minds; the spirit of the law governs our hearts.

Love is the fulfilling of the law. (Romans 13:10, italics added)

To instruct us in the whole law of love, our Father gave us two primary teaching aids to sharpen our understanding and conviction. The first is his *written instructions* that define his laws for life and godliness; the second is a *spiritual illustration* that shows us how to fulfill those laws. Again, God's written instructions are called the Ten Commandments and his simple illustration for fulfilling his commandments is called the pattern.[124]

The Ten Commandments teach us the *letter of the law* to refine our understanding. His pattern teaches us the *spirit of the law* to refine our performance. The letter of the law governs our minds; the spirit of the law governs our hearts. Like male and female genders, the letter and the spirit complement one another, but they are not the same. For example, the letter of the law emphatically states "*thou shalt not kill,*" but the spirit of the law quietly affirms, "*I give my life for you.*" Both parts of the law are necessary to fulfill the whole law of love with its hard judgments and its tender mercies.

Accordingly, if we were to ignore the spirit of the law and focus on the letter only, it would bind us to a miserable life of legalism— "Touch not; taste not; handle not" (Colossians 2:21). Paul touched on this grievous outcome when he told the church at Corinth, "*The letter kills, but the Spirit gives life*" (2 Corinthians 3:6, NKJV, italics added). But the natural man couldn't fully grasp the spirit of the law, because he was carnally minded—not spiritually minded. Paul told the Roman church that "the carnal mind is enmity against God: for it is not subject to the law of God, neither indeed can be" (8:7). He wrote, "To be carnally minded is death; but to be spiritually minded is life and peace" (Romans 8:6).

It's because the law is spiritual and we are carnal that we were so easily sold under sin,[125] because, as previously mentioned, to be carnally minded is to be focused on self. So the carnal man has always struggled to consistently uphold the spirit of the law, because the spirit of the law has always been focused on others,[126] namely, *I give my life for you.*

> Both parts of the law are necessary to fulfill the whole law of love with its hard judgments and its tender mercies.

Even though Adam understood the basic difference between right and wrong,[127] his inability to grasp the spirit of the law and consistently walk in love is what gave rise to the veil protecting God's heart. But again, God's workmanship in mankind wasn't finished in Eden,[128] it couldn't be finished until we were created in Christ Jesus and sanctified for entry within the veil.

For by one offering He has perfected forever those who are *being* sanctified [prepared-made holy]. (Hebrews 10:14, NKJV, italics added)

Our omniscient Father's plan from the very beginning was to form his divine nature within us through the faithfulness of Jesus the Christ, his firstborn Son, so that Jesus could be preeminent in all things[129] and we could be glorified with him.[130] To do this, our Father would use the letter of the law to convict us of our need for change and then provide our way for change through the faithfulness of his Son.

To accomplish this magnificent objective, our Father began with defining his laws for life and godliness through his servant Moses, and then he empowered our hearts to uphold them through his Son, Jesus the Christ. Defining his law was easy enough, God just wrote his commandments on tablets of stone with his finger (see Exodus 31:18). But empowering our hearts to consistently uphold his law is a totally different story.

The standard of love God set forth through the letter of the law compels us to resist and twist it, because to love our neighbor as we love ourselves is contrary to the carnal mind-set of our natural man. Again, by yielding his will to God's in Gethsemane, Jesus showed us that to yield our will to the will of God is the first step to overcoming our carnal nature, the first step to life and godliness, and the first step toward true reconciliation with God and others.

We have been given the freedom of choice, giving us the liberty to follow our will, which is the heart of the matter. It's the heart of the challenge to transform our nature into the likeness of God's, because it's not even close to being compatible with his first and second commandments. It can't be compatible because the carnal mind is focused on self, whereas the spiritual mind is focused on others.[131] So to form the nature of Christ within us, we must be born again of God's Spirit to even discern his will and then be persuaded through time, experience, and the tutelage of the Holy Spirit that his will is better than ours.

> ...the carnal mind is focused on self, whereas the spiritual mind is focused on others.

Jesus knew the Father before the world was and was persuaded God's will was best. But for us to exercise his level of faith in God, we must be persuaded too. Paul said he was persuaded (see Romans

8:38–39), and now, after seventy years of successes and failures, I am persuaded too. Through experience, the word of God has persuaded me that his ways are higher than mine, but that's certainly not the end of the matter. I still have to make daily choices to put off the former conduct of the old man and put on a new man, created in righteousness and true holiness (see Ephesians 4:20–24). Paul made this even clearer when he wrote, "Let not sin therefore reign in your mortal body, that ye should obey it in the lusts thereof" (Romans 6:12).

...our journey toward unblemished communion with God or others begins with the first frightful step of a faithfully yielded will.

Therefore, in the likeness of Christ in Gethsemane, our journey toward unblemished communion with God or others begins with the first frightful step of a faithfully yielded will. This is where the hard work of true reconciliation begins—we need to yield our will and consign our old ways to the altar of sacrifice, in the footsteps of Christ, and that is not even close to a natural act.

Two Mountains

God has called us from two mountains: the blazing fires of *Mount Sinai* where both the law of love and his pattern for fulfilling the law were given to us through Moses,[132] and then from the searing heat of *Mount Moriah*[133] where Jerusalem was built and God's Lamb was slain to fulfill the law of love for us. Our Father called us to walk in love from Mount Sinai and then he sent his Son to lead the way on Mount Moriah. This is the reason Jesus told us to follow him. He led our way from a yielded will in the garden of Gethsemane to the cross of Calvary and onward to God's holiest place in the heavens by following the pattern's requirements—step by step.

At least seventeen times in the four gospels of Matthew, Mark, Luke, and John, Jesus said "follow me," which means we are called to go where he goes and do what he does. But to follow him, we must know *where* he was going and know *how* to follow him—hence the pattern's instructions.

> Our Father called us to walk in love from Mount Sinai and then he sent his Son to lead the way on Mount Moriah.

There are no other works reported in Scripture that will secure our acceptance in God's holiest place except the works of following Christ through the pattern's requirements with faith in his atoning sacrifice. It's how we return God's love and fulfill our role in the ministry of reconciliation. Jesus said "he" is the one we need to follow and that anyone who attempts to enter in some other way is merely a thief and a robber (see John 10:1). In view of these facts, I must accept that God's *commandments* are our objective, his *pattern* is our directive

> God's commandments are our objective, his pattern is our directive.

He that overcometh shall inherit all things; and I will be his God, and he shall be my son. (Revelation 21:7)

A Final Note

As previously stated, several times, long before God's binary instructions were given from Mount Sinai and long before the foundation of the world was laid, our omniscient heavenly Father had already purposed to create us in Christ Jesus. So God's workmanship in us cannot be finished until we faithfully follow Christ through the pattern's instructions for our sanctification to transform our nature from the carnal to the divine and return God's love with an unblemished heart and be glorified together

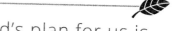

God's plan for us is a lot like building a car, first the inner mechanics and then the body work.

with Christ. How else can we rise in new and glorious bodies for face-to-face communion with the Creator of heaven and earth, the holy One whose nature is love? God's plan for us is a lot like building a car, first the inner mechanics and then the body work. So let's take a closer look at God's heavenly pattern.

And ye are *complete in him* [Jesus], which is the head of all principality and power. (Colossians 2:10, italics added)

Hear, ye children, *the instruction of a father*, and attend to know understanding. For *I give you good doctrine*, forsake ye not my law.

PROVERBS 4:1–2, ITALICS ADDED

Let this mind be in you, which was also in Christ Jesus.

PHILIPPIANS 2:5

19

The Heavenly Pattern

Moses was admonished of God when he was about to make the tabernacle: for, See, saith he, that *thou make all things according to the pattern* shewed to thee in the mount.

HEBREWS 8:5, ITALICS ADDED

> It's the only religion in the world that's about God reaching down to initiate a spiritual connection with man through grace, so we could return his standard of love through faith.

While returning to Florida from the Bahamas, my airplane suddenly lost all electrical power and its navigational aids shut down. I had to continue across the ocean on dead reckoning alone. Dead reckoning can be less than an exact science due to variable winds, pilot error, and the magnetic deviation of the compass. Getting to Florida was easy enough, just head due west, but a direct course to the airport of entry for clearing customs had become crucial due to low fuel reserves.

In contrast to dead reckoning by a compass, our current navigational abilities with modern-day electronics make almost every

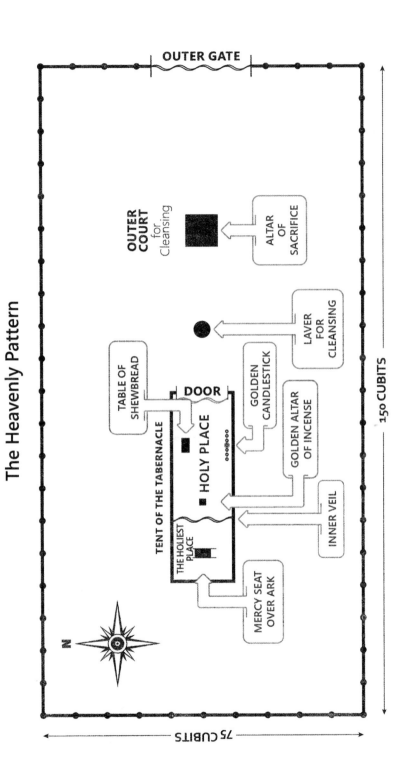

The Heavenly Pattern

OUTER GATE

OUTER COURT
for Cleansing

ALTAR OF SACRIFICE

LAVER FOR CLEANSING

TABLE OF SHEWBREAD

DOOR

HOLY PLACE

GOLDEN CANDLESTICK

GOLDEN ALTAR OF INCENSE

TENT OF THE TABERNACLE

INNER VEIL

THE HOLIEST PLACE

MERCY SEAT OVER ARK

N

150 CUBITS

75 CUBITS

pilot look like a skilled navigator: the more precise our information, the more precise our ability to plot a straight and narrow course to our intended destination. If you've ever been low on fuel over the ocean, with fuel gauges flashing on empty, then you understand how important a direct course can be.

As repeatedly stated, our Father has commanded his blessing of everlasting life on unity (see Psalm 133), but he didn't give us this extraordinary command without showing us how to sustain unity, which, of course, is why he gave us the pattern. But even with God's simple instructions for walking in love, no one could build their end of the spiritual connection to God's exacting standards because of the limitations of their carnal mind. The carnal mind is not subject to the law of God and it cannot be, because its very nature is at enmity with God.[134] So God sent his Son to do for us what we could not do for ourselves—to sanctify us for the spiritual connection.

> For both He who sanctifies [Jesus] and those who are *being sanctified* [us] are all of one, for which reason He is not ashamed to call them brethren. (Hebrews 2:11, NKJV, italics added)

This is what makes Christianity profoundly unique. It's the only religion in the world that's about God reaching down to initiate a spiritual connection with man through grace, so we could return his standard of love through faith.[135] Returning God's love by obeying the pattern's instructions for walking in his love is how faith works. It is how we fulfill God's first and second commandments to love with all our hearts. Paul wrote, "Love worketh no ill to his neighbour: therefore love is the fulfilling of the law" (Romans 13:10).

Christianity is the only religion in the world where God has provided a simple set of instructions for reconciliation with him through spiritual sanctification. His pattern gives us step-by-step instructions for preparing our hearts for unblemished communion, so we can fly a direct course to the secret place of his soul and even to the souls of those he's made in his image. Then, at the appointed time for our creation in Christ Jesus, our Father did for us what we could not do for ourselves—he sent his Son to lead us through the pattern's requirements.

God has surrendered his heart to ours through Christ, so we could surrender our hearts to his through Christ.[136] So putting our faith in the cleansing blood of Jesus's sacrifice and following him through the pattern's requirements for communion is what the gospel is all about, it's how we work the works of God (see John 6:28–29)—it's our faith in action. God's pattern charts our course through the narrow way to life with God and one another, to secure his blessing of life forevermore through unity. The bottom line is, God gave us his pattern to show us how to be one with him and then he sent his Son to lead us through it. Now the onus is on us to follow him.

> God has surrendered his heart to ours through Christ, so we could surrender our hearts to his through Christ.

> The bottom line is, God gave us his pattern to show us how to be one with him and then he sent his Son to lead us through it. Now the onus is on us to follow him.

And this is love, that we walk after his commandments. (2 John 1:6)

From before the beginning of creation, our omniscient Father understood an unchangeable truth: to have a faultless connection between two hearts, both hearts need to be faultless. Jude clearly confirmed God's divine objective when he told us Christ is going to present us faultless before the presence of God's glory (1:24). When I think about this passage in Jude, I have to ask, what righteous father who had a faultless heart wouldn't have this same goal for his children—the goal of sanctifying their hearts for a faultless connection with him?

...to have a faultless connection between two hearts, both hearts need to be faultless.

God's pattern is his divine blueprint for securing a faultless connection with us. Its requirements were met by his Son to complete the bridge of hearts, and it's to be used by us to secure the benefits of the bridge.

God's blueprint was first used for building the tabernacle in the wilderness and then used again for building the temples in Jerusalem, but these earthly illustrations were only examples and shadows of the things Jesus would do to lead our way into heavenly places (see Hebrews 8:5). They were given to show us the way Christ would go to sanctify his heart for communion with God after becoming our sin, and the way we must go to follow him.

For he [the Father] hath made him [Jesus] to be sin for us, who knew no sin; that we might be made the righteousness of God in him. (2 Corinthians 5:21)

As we look at the upcoming chapters, we will soon learn the pattern's three requirements for reconciliation are one and the same with the three dynamics of agapao love. According to *Merriam-Webster's Collegiate Dictionary*, Eleventh Edition, a dynamic is "an underlying cause of change or growth." So when God's pattern directs us to

Its requirements were met by his Son to complete the bridge of hearts, and it's to be used by us to secure the benefits of the bridge.

perform the three dynamics of agapao love, it is requiring us to make the changes we need for spiritual growth from the carnal mind that's focused on self—the old man—to the spiritual mind that's focused on others—the new man who's created in Christ Jesus.

The pattern's three dynamics require us to cleanse, renew, and surrender our hearts, so we can develop the right spirit within us and build our spiritual connections on a faithful, true, and trustworthy heart. This is the process of sanctification our Father has called us to. And this we must do, if we want to become one with him and others in his eternal kingdom, because the kingdom of God is not an external location, the kingdom of God is within us (see Luke 17:21).

> ...the pattern's three requirements for reconciliation are one and the same with the three dynamics of agapao love.

Again, the first and foremost problem people like me have with this change of heart is to forsake the former conduct of the old man, requiring our old man to die. So let's move in for a closer look at the pattern's three dynamics for change and growth—for crucifying our old man and renewing a right spirit within us.

Knowing this, that *our old man is crucified with him [Christ]*, that the body of sin might be destroyed, that henceforth we should not serve sin. (Romans 6:6, italics added)

Let not sin therefore reign in your mortal body, that ye should obey it in the lusts thereof.

ROMANS 6:12

Therefore if any man be in Christ, he is a new creature: old things are passed away; behold, all things are become new.

2 CORINTHIANS 5:17

My little children, of whom I travail in birth again until Christ be formed in you.

GALATIANS 4:19

Christ in you, the hope of glory.

COLOSSIANS 1:27

20

The Pattern's Three Dynamics 🍃

And they overcame him [Satan] by the blood of the Lamb [spiritual cleansing], and by the word of their testimony [spiritual renewal]; and they loved not their lives unto the death [spiritual surrender].

REVELATION 12:11

When I began learning to fly, I didn't understand the principles of flight, so the law of aerodynamics mentally challenged me. Aerodynamics is the study of the motion of air, particularly when it interacts with a solid object such as an airplane wing. It's the science dealing with forces acting on bodies in motion to create lift.

I once thought the wing of an airplane glided on air much like a boat glides on water. I was wrong—totally wrong. Airplane wings are curved on the top and flat on the bottom, making the distance over the top greater than the distance under the bottom. Because of this, the air flows faster over the curved top than it does under the straight, flat bottom. This difference between the required speeds of air across the longer distance on the top and shorter distance on the bottom causes the pressure on the top of the wing to be less than the pressure on the bottom, and this higher pressure underneath the wing creates an upward force called lift. Lift keeps the airplane from falling from the sky.

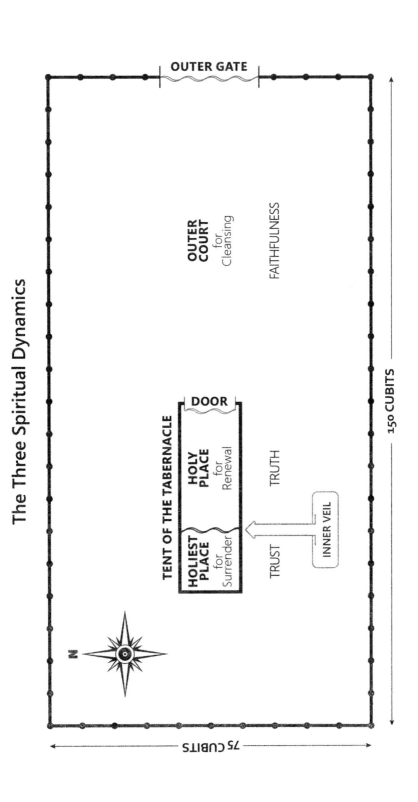

The Three Spiritual Dynamics

OUTER GATE

OUTER COURT
for Cleansing

FAITHFULNESS

TENT OF THE TABERNACLE

DOOR

HOLY PLACE
for Renewal

HOLIEST PLACE
for Surrender

TRUTH

TRUST

INNER VEIL

N

150 CUBITS

75 CUBITS

It took time for me to believe and accept the law of aerodynamics, because it didn't align with my previous assumptions. In a similar fashion, it took time for me to believe and accept that the pattern's three requirements are the three dynamics of agapao love. Just as I was once skeptical of how aerodynamics created the upward forces of lift in flight, I was even more skeptical of how the pattern's three dynamics created the upward forces of lift in love. The course of action they set didn't align with my previous assumptions about how to finish my course with joy, especially the part about sacrifice.

> ...these three dynamics will create the upward forces of lift in the mystery of life we call love.

But I soon learned the three dynamics of the pattern were for building timeless spiritual connections so we could soar to the highest reaches of life and love without crashing and burning. And as we shall affirm and reaffirm in the coming chapters, the pattern's three dynamics work in unison to build faithful, true, and trustworthy hearts. But in this and the next chapter, my goal is not to look at how to build the bridge, it's to name and identify the three components of the bridge: To identify the three dynamics of the pattern that perform agapao love and the seven steps that perform them.

> We must cleanse our hearts in the outer court and then renew our hearts in the holy place before we can surrender a sanctified heart to God and others...

You, too, may find the pattern's dynamics contrary to your previous assumptions, but in real life, I can testify from seventy years of living and learning, these three dynamics will create the upward forces of lift in the mystery of life we call love. It may take some time to understand and accept these dynamics as the right components for building our bridges, but we must learn to trust them, because their origins are from that everlasting source we call Father.

The Pattern's First Dynamic: Cleansing the Heart of All Unfaithfulness

Be thou faithful unto death and I will give thee a crown of life. (Revelation 2:10)

The first dynamic of agapao love is faithfulness. It's accomplished in the outer court—on the outside of the tabernacle tent—through sacrifice and washing. The sole requirement of this dynamic is to faithfully cleanse the heart of all unrighteousness before entering the first room of the tent.

Sacrifice cleanses the heart of all unfaithfulness in order to establish a faithful heart. So the first dynamic of the pattern is to establish faithfulness, because faithfulness is the rock we build our spiritual connections on. Therefore, the altar for sacrifice and the laver for washing were located front and center in the tabernacle court where they must be dealt with before entering the tabernacle tent. Faithfulness is the first and foremost requirement of the pattern, because it is the first and foremost requirement of agapao love. We must be cleansed of all unfaithfulness in the court, before we can enter the first room of the tabernacle tent called the holy place, to be renewed with the right spirit.

> Sacrifice cleanses the heart of all unfaithfulness in order to establish a faithful heart.

I will even betroth thee unto me in faithfulness: and thou shalt know the Lord. (Hosea 2:20)

The Pattern's Second Dynamic: Renewing the Heart with the Right Spirit

Create in me a *clean heart*, O God; and renew a *right spirit* within me. (Psalm 51:10, italics added)

After faithfully cleansing our hearts in the court, the second dynamic of agapao love is to be renewed with the right Spirit in the cleansed heart. This is accomplished in the first room of the tabernacle tent—the holy place. We must cleanse our hearts in the outer court and then renew our hearts in the holy place before we can surrender a sanctified heart to God and others for unblemished communion. Lighting the seven lamps of the golden lampstand in the holy place of the tent was symbolic of renewing our hearts with the seven Spirits of God and Christ, and, of course, the seven Spirits of God would be the right Spirit to form within us for true communion with God the Father and God the Son.

As to the Seven Spirits of God

There were seven lamps of fire burning before the throne, which are *the seven Spirits of God.* (Revelation 4:5, italics added)

As to the Seven Spirits of God in Christ

These things saith he [Christ] *that hath the seven Spirits of God.* (Revelation 3:1, italics added)

We will look at the possible identities of these seven Spirits in coming chapters. But for now, to gain a better understanding of how the seven Spirits of God compose his nature, I would compare them to the seven facets of light. Just as one light is collectively composed of seven different wavelengths, God's Holy Spirit is collectively composed of seven different Spirits. And the great news of the gospel is, our Father is forming all seven facets of his light in the hearts of those who love him to make us his children of light.

Ye are all the children of light, and the children of the day: we are not of the night, nor of darkness. (1 Thessalonians 5:5)

The Pattern's Third Dynamic: Surrendering a Trustworthy Heart

As for God, his way is perfect: the word of the Lord is tried: he is *a buckler to all those that trust in him.* (Psalm 18:30, italics added)

The *first dynamic* of agapao love is cleansing the heart of all unfaithfulness. The *second dynamic* is renewing the right spirit in our cleansed heart. This *third and final dynamic* of the pattern is surrendering the heart. Surrendering a cleansed and renewed heart establishes trust. Faithfulness is the rock we build on, truth is the substance we build with, and trust is the span we must build to perfect our spiritual connections.

> Faithfulness is the rock we build on, truth is the substance we build with, and trust is the span we must build to perfect our spiritual connections.

Establishing a trustworthy connection is the last requirement of the pattern, which is why it's accomplished in the last room of the tabernacle tent—the holiest place. The holiest place is where the mercy seat is located. It's where the cleansed and renewed heart can be surrendered for mercy and acceptance by the Spirit within. And it must be accepted by the Spirit within before he will remove his veil to complete the spiritual connection.

Much like a treasure map to unlimited resources, God's pattern charts our course through the narrow way that leads to life, so we can find our life in God. And I am convinced by my seventy trips around the sun that any person who rejects God's instructions for building spiritual bridges will never soar to the high and lofty places of the One who inhabits eternity. But if we follow our forerunner through the pattern's dynamics with faith in his blood for our cleansing, we can meet the three requirements of love that will perfect our reconciliation with him. And this we must do, so we won't just drift through a moment of flight on this turbulent planet, and then, like a vapor, simply vanish away.

For what is your life? It is even a vapor that appears for a little time and then vanishes away. (James 4:14, NKJV)

Not that I have already obtained all this,
or have already arrived at my goal, but I press on to take hold
of that for which Christ Jesus took hold of me.

PHILIPPIANS 3:12, NIV

According as he [God the Father] hath chosen us in him [God the Son]
before the foundation of the world, that *we should be holy
and without blame before him in love.*

EPHESIANS 1:4, ITALICS ADDED

Of his own will begat he us with the word of truth, that we should be
a kind of firstfruits of his creatures.

JAMES 1:18, ITALICS ADDED

21

The Pattern's Seven Steps 🍃

For even hereunto were ye called: because Christ also suffered for
us, leaving us an example, that *ye should follow his steps*.

1 PETER 2:21, ITALICS ADDED

There are seven steps for performing the pattern's three
dynamics. The first step is spiritual attraction and the last or
seventh step is spiritual communion. Spiritual attraction is the
call that draws us to the heart of another and spiritual communion is
the goal of the call. In between the pattern's first and seventh steps
are three heart-changing dynamics for perfecting agapao love. Again,
these three dynamics are cleansing, renewing, and surrendering our
hearts to build faithful, true, and trustworthy hearts.

Jesus yielded his will and became our sins to cleanse us and set us
free, then he met the pattern's three dynamics to obtain *the joy that
God had set before him*, and now we are called to do the same, to yield
our will and follow Christ through the pattern's three dynamics for
the joy that God has set before us. Our heavenly Father, who gave to
us the ministry of reconciliation, has set the same joy before us that
he set before Christ, which is to be glorified together, to be seated
at God's communion table with Christ and many brethren. But to

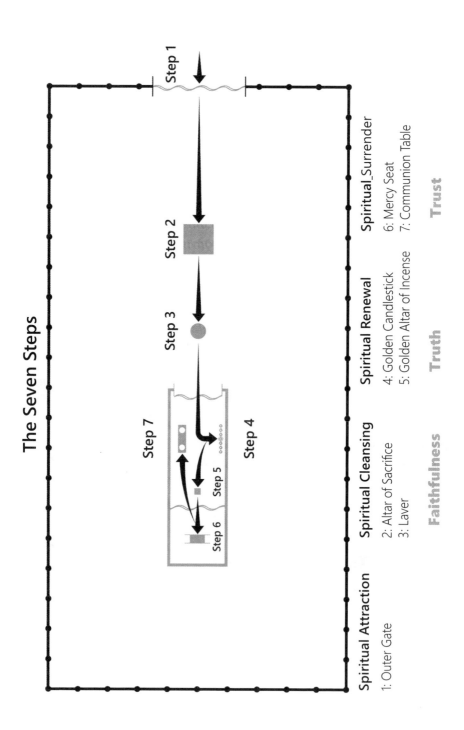

The Seven Steps

Step 1

Step 2

Step 3

Step 7

Step 5

Step 6

Step 4

Spiritual Attraction	Spiritual Cleansing	Spiritual Renewal	Spiritual_Surrender
1: Outer Gate	2: Altar of Sacrifice	4: Golden Candlestick	6: Mercy Seat
	3: Laver	5: Golden Altar of Incense	7: Communion Table
Faithfulness	**Truth**		**Trust**

follow in the footsteps of Jesus and secure that highest goal, we must take the same steps Jesus took.

Looking unto Jesus the author and finisher of our faith; who for the joy that was set before him endured the cross. (Hebrews 12:2)

My dear friend Al used to humorously muse over a satirical quote hanging on the wall where he worked, because it aptly addressed our reluctance to take the necessary steps for change. It read something like this, "Insanity is doing the same thing over and over and expecting different results." For me, that exasperating sign was up close and personal. I loved my old nature, so I didn't want to change a thing. The problem was, I needed different results.

> The problem was, I needed different results.

Actually, I don't think I'm alone with this problem. I tend to believe there are many people who resist checking the video port of their minds against God's instructions for life and godliness. By our continued resistance, we remain just as we are—stuck in our previous malady of missing the mark. It's more consistent with our carnal nature to pick up the prayer line and lambaste the divine manufacturer with complaints about our defects, slam down the line, and head to the local candy store for some coveted self-indulgence. But there may well be a colossal outburst of personal humiliation when we walk out the door at the end of the age with our great big hat in our trembling little hands, wishing we had listened to our forerunner's plea to take up our cross and follow him.

Jesus repeatedly called us to follow him. But if truth be told, his call seemed a little ambiguous to me. When I was younger, I didn't have a clue how to follow Christ because I didn't know anything about where he was going or how he was getting there. I had the same questions Thomas had when he asked Jesus, *Where* are you going, and *how* do I follow you?[137] So I began to search Scripture for some answers.

The answer to *where Jesus was going* was made clear when I discovered he was headed to the holiest place of God in the heavens to reconcile our hearts with God's, after he had become the sins of our world.[138] The answer to *how to follow him* was made clear when I realized he followed the pattern's instructions for cleansing, renewing, and surrendering his heart so he would be accepted in God's holiest place. Once I understood *where* Jesus was going and *how* he was getting there, it became clear that following the pattern's instructions for spiritual sanctification was how I followed him.

> ...following the pattern's instructions for spiritual sanctification was how I followed him.

I was surprised to learn that God's pattern was his blueprint for building spiritual bridges and that it was the blueprint Jesus used to connect the lifeline from the living God who loves man to the dying man who loves God. Once I realized the pattern was used for building the spiritual connection from God's heart to man's, I also realized its three dynamics would work for rebuilding my relationships. It showed me how to build new bridges with my wife, my family, my friends, and my neighbors as well as my God. Learning the pattern's three dynamics and seven steps gave me the right direction, but I still had to choose to follow its instructions, that is, if I wanted to walk where Jesus walked in his ministry of reconciliation.

> ...it was the blueprint Jesus used to connect the lifeline from the living God who loves man to the dying man who loves God.

If our eyes are on the prize of the high calling of God in Christ Jesus, then we must take the seven steps that Jesus took to capture the joy that God has set before all of us. So before looking at these steps in detail, I'd like to briefly list them in the order the Levite priests took them, which is the same the order Jesus took them.

Then said Jesus unto his disciples, If any man will come after me, let him deny himself, and take up his cross, and follow me. (Matthew 16:24)

The Pattern's Seven Steps

1. First, he responded to God's call and *yielded his will* in Gethsemane—**outer gate.**

2. Second, *he sacrificed his all* at the cross of Calvary—**altar.**

3. Third, he *purified his heart* in the waters of God's word—**laver.**

4. Fourth, he *renewed his heart* with the seven Spirits of God—**golden candlestick.**

5. Fifth, he *petitioned God* for the forgiveness of man—**golden altar of incense.**

6. Sixth, he *surrendered his lifeblood* for the surety of man's cleansing—**mercy seat.**

7. Seventh, he *became one with God*, sharing the bread of faces (shewbread)—**communion table.**

We cannot follow Christ without faith in the blood of his sacrifice for our cleansing. It is the only way for the carnal man to meet the divine requirements of righteousness so we can follow our forerunner with boldness. But if we do put our faith in the blood of God's Lamb who died for us, took our sins to the grave, and imputed his righteousness to us, we can follow his lead through the remainder of the pattern and boldly go to that mystical place where no man had gone before—the holiest place of the heart of God.

Having therefore, brethren, boldness to enter into the holiest
by the blood of Jesus.

HEBREWS 10:19

Be ye therefore followers of God, as dear children;
And walk in love, as Christ also hath loved us, and hath given himself
for us an offering and a sacrifice to God.

EPHESIANS 5:1–2

Which hope we have as an anchor of the soul, both sure and steadfast,
and which entereth into that within the veil; Whither the forerunner is
for us entered, even Jesus.

(HEBREWS 6:19–20)

For we have not an high priest which cannot be touched with the
feeling of our infirmities; but was in all points tempted like as we are,
yet without sin.

HEBREWS 4:15, ITALICS ADDED

Let us therefore come boldly unto the throne of grace, that we may
obtain mercy, and find grace to help in time of need.

HEBREWS 4:16

Not my will, but thine.

LUKE 22:42

22

Validating the Pattern 🌿

I have seen you in the sanctuary and beheld your power and your
glory. Because your love is better than life,
my lips will glorify you.

PSALM 63:2–3, NIV

nder disastrous circumstances in the wilderness of Judea, an
inhospitable environment, David wrote the above verses and
said he'd seen God in his
sanctuary. I'm quite convinced
this was a natural metaphor of a
spiritual encounter. David certainly
didn't see God's face with his
natural eyes, because no natural
man can see God's *face* and live (see
Exodus 33:20). But there is clear
record that many have seen God's
tangible *Spirit* in his sanctuary and
lived to tell the story.

🌿

...both structures
were immediately
accepted by the
visible appearance
of the Holy Spirit
on the day of their
dedications.

By looking at the historical record of the pattern, we will discover
how important the pattern is to the Spirit who resides in its holiest
place—the Holy Spirit of God. What has truly set the pattern

apart as a uniquely supreme teaching aid, completely unrivaled in the chronicles of mankind is, it is the blueprint for the only two structures that were ever built by the hands of men and then publicly endorsed by the Spirit of God. These two structures are the *tabernacle in the wilderness* and *Solomon's temple in Jerusalem.*

> God uses natural things to teach us spiritual things, because we are natural men in a natural world who best learn through natural illustrations.

Both structures were built to the pattern's design and both are extremely significant in the chronicles of Scripture because they show us the proper protocol for following Christ. Therefore, it is important to note that both structures were immediately accepted by the visible appearance of the Holy Spirit on the day of their dedications. On that special day, God's Spirit visibly entered the holiest place of these two structures so he could dwell among the people and commune with them from his mercy seat (see Exodus 25:22). Again, the tabernacle and the temple are the only man-made dwellings God has ever publicly endorsed by the tangible habitation of his Spirit, as told below.

The dedication of the tabernacle in the wilderness

A cloud covered the tent of the congregation, and *the glory of the Lord filled the tabernacle.* And Moses was not able to enter into the tent of the congregation, because the cloud abode thereon, and the glory of the Lord filled the tabernacle.

(Exodus 40:34–35, italics added)

The dedication of Solomon's temple in Jerusalem

And it came to pass, when the priests were come out of the holy place, that the cloud filled the house of the Lord, So that the priests could not stand to minister because of the cloud: *for the glory of the Lord had filled the house of the Lord.* (1 Kings 8:10–11, italics added)

God had the Jews build these earthly paradigms for three well-known reasons. First, so he could dwell among them and teach them how to be accepted in his holiest place. Second, so he could show all men the way our forerunner would go for a full reconciliation with God after becoming the sins of our world. Third, so he could show us the way we must go to follow him. God uses natural things to teach us spiritual things, because we are natural men in a natural world who best learn through natural illustrations.

There are millions of Jews who literally saw God's Spirit when he accepted the tabernacle in the wilderness many centuries before David was born. And there are many more who saw God's Spirit descend on Solomon's temple, only a few years after David died. As a newborn nation of slaves in the wilderness of Sinai, Israel saw the tangible Spirit of God amid their camp every day, and then centuries later in Jerusalem's golden age, they saw him again in the City of David. These ancient declarations preserved in Scripture still bear witness to us today. They validate that the purpose of the pattern was for building unblemished spiritual connections between God and man.

Proper Protocol

In the days of old, on that special day of the year called Yom Kippur, or the Day of Atonement, the Levite high priest would sanctify himself for entering God's holiest place by following the pattern's instructions. His objective being to prepare himself for taking the blood of *the national sacrifice* to God's mercy seat where he would atone for the sins of the people. The sacrifice had to be a pure sacrifice, without spot or blemish, for the blood to be accepted and the connection to be unblemished. If the priest didn't follow all the pattern's instructions for his own sanctification, he would not be accepted in God's holiest place and could even be slain.[139] Therefore, the entry of the high priest to atone for the sins of the people required careful attention to the pattern's protocol. Again, this priestly action of the Levites mirrored the coming ministry of Jesus the Christ, our true High Priest, who took the blood of his sacrifice to God's mercy seat and reconciled us to God through an unblemished connection by meeting the pattern's requirements.

God gave us his Ten Commandments to show us what to do, and then he gave us the pattern to show us how to do it, and now we have a God-given role to follow his Son through the pattern's instructions for our ministry of reconciliation.

Wherefore in all things it behoved him [Christ Jesus] to be made like unto his brethren, that he might be a merciful and faithful high priest in things pertaining to God, *to make reconciliation for the sins of the people.* (Hebrews 2:17 italics added)

Today, God's protocol for approaching his holiest place hasn't changed at all. But there have been two important changes in man's role that we should carefully note. The *first* is, our one sacrifice for sin has already been made by Jesus the Christ—God's Lamb—so no other sacrifice is needed except those of a broken and contrite heart (Psalm 51:17). Therefore, anyone and everyone who puts their faith in the Lamb's blood for their cleansing can safely and effectively proceed beyond the altar to continue their journey toward the holiest place of God with boldness. The *second* is, we don't have to go alone. After putting our faith in the Lamb's blood for our cleansing, he will lead us as our shepherd through the pattern's dynamics to make us God's vessels of honor, to make us a faultless people who are sanctified for the Master's use and prepared for every good work (see 2 Timothy 2:21).

God gave us his Ten Commandments to show us *what to do*, and then he gave us the pattern to show us *how to do it*, and now we have a God-given role to follow his Son through the pattern's instructions for our ministry of reconciliation. We must put our faith in the blood of Christ that was shed for our cleansing, and then follow his lead through spiritual renewal and surrender, so we too can find the way, the straight and narrow way, the only way that leads to the abundant life in the heart of God. God's way is straight, his pattern is exact, and all who would attempt to enter some other way are merely thieves and robbers.

I tell you the truth, the man who does not enter the sheep pen by the gate, but climbs in by some other way, is a thief and a robber.

JOHN 10:1, NIV

For the Messiah did not enter a sanctuary made with hands
but into heaven itself, so that He might now appear
in the presence of God for us.

HEBREWS 9:24, HCSB

O Lord, the hope of Israel, all that forsake thee shall be ashamed,
and they that depart from me shall be written in the earth, because
they have forsaken the Lord, the fountain of living waters.

JEREMIAH 17:13

Section VII—Building the Bridge of Hearts

Not every one that saith unto me, Lord,
Lord, shall enter into the kingdom of heaven;
but he that doeth the will of my Father which is in heaven.

MATTHEW 7:21

23

Step One: Spiritual Attraction 🍃

No man can come to me [Jesus], except the Father
which hath sent me draw him.

JOHN 6:44

The Chinese sage Lao-tzu well said, "The journey of a thousand miles begins with the first step." The spiritual journey into the holiest place of God is no different. To successfully make this journey, we must take the first step of the pattern by responding to the call of God's Spirit. Just as another person's spirit must attract our spirit before we can begin to develop our connection with them, the first step toward God's holiest place can only be made when his Spirit draws us. In the passage above Jesus told us, "No man can come to me, except the Father which hath sent me draw him" (John 6:44), so let's take a closer look at the call.

We have all sensed the call of our spirit to another's heart and theirs to ours. We are drawn by reason of God's design, because we were made for the intimate bond of spiritual unity with the Father and the Son. God made us in his three-person image, so we could relate to each other in the same three ways he relates to us—physically, intellectually, and spiritually—body, soul, and spirit.[140] God has a tangible body,[141] God has a soul,[142] and God is a Spirit,[143] so each of

Step One: Spiritual Attraction

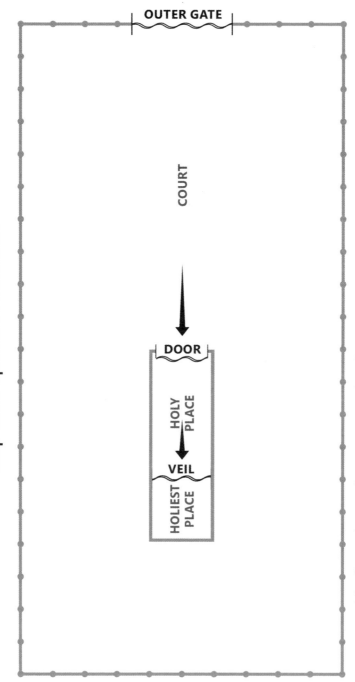

OUTER GATE

COURT

DOOR

HOLY PLACE

VEIL

HOLIEST PLACE

The four colors on his outer gate, the tabernacle door, and his inner veil were blue, purple, and scarlet threads on finely twined linen.

these three parts of the whole has been built into our constitution, enabling us to attract and interact with one another in the same three ways he can attract and interact with us. Therefore, being made in his image, we can operate with all three parts collectively or with each part independently.

For example, we can be *physically* attracted to another's body without connecting on the same intellectual or spiritual plane. We can also connect *intellectually* without the slightest hint of physical or spiritual magnetism. And we can also be drawn to another's *spirit* without intellectual or physical interaction. These three parts of our whole can each function independently and can be powerful and pleasurable in their own right. But our three parts can also function collectively for the total union of body, soul, and spirit, which, of course, is the highest of goals.

When I think about the ability of each part to function independently, I recall certain experiences that further substantiate the unique role of each. For example, I have felt the immediate acceptance or rejection of another's spirit the moment I've met them; I've also sensed my immediate acceptance or rejection of theirs. But when I consider the shallow waters of physical attraction, I'm often reminded of my first day in the second grade.

She was not only beautiful, but her desk sat right in front of mine. Wow, this had to be providence, or at least good luck. Either way, I was happy about it. I don't know about you, but I was capable of love at first sight in my earliest years of Sunday school—maybe even before then. So by the time I hit second grade, I was an old hand at romantic procedures. It may have taken a few hours to work up the courage, but eventually, I was able to express my deep love for this beautiful girl by thumping her on the head with my pencil.

Obviously, she was new to romance and didn't understand a boy's deep affection for a girl when it came her way. Why did she cry? But an even more puzzling question was, why did she betray my love when the teacher asked her why she was crying? I hadn't realized there could be people in this world who weren't as advanced in the art of romantic expression as I was. But after an hour or two in the corner, I figured it out.

When I think back to the lost romances in my life, I suspect I wasn't as advanced in the art of love as I had once thought. And now, after seventy years of living and occasionally learning, I've put my charming pencil down, picked up my irritating computer, and started writing about the more important matters of the heart—matters that address my deeper understanding of love and how to manage its attractions (and distractions) without causing tears. When God's instructions are faithfully followed, these important matters of the heart can lead us to the highest bond of unity through that mysterious power of a mutual spiritual attraction.

Spiritual attraction is what constrained me to stay in those Rocky Mountains and compose this work. I'm attracted to the holy nature of the One who has drawn me by his Spirit and of whom I believe led me to that isolated place. God's love is much deeper than words, beyond information, and his loving-kindness is far more desirable than the fleeting attractions of the shiny things in our world. Those who respond to the call of God's Spirit have an ever-increasing longing to know him completely, face to face, through the mutual correlation of body, soul, and spirit. I am learning that just one moment with the Spirit of God has more of the substance of paradise than any pencil lover could ever inscribe on the memoirs of the human heart. And the great news is, I never need an eraser.

> It's a core power that radiates from within the heart to draw spiritual beings to spiritual beings.

What is this powerful force called spiritual attraction? It's a core power that radiates from within the heart to draw spiritual beings to spiritual beings. It mysteriously glows from deep within us to outwardly reveal our inner nature to others, and if our nature is appealing to theirs, it incites a spiritual response from deep within their heart. So when the attraction is mutual, it draws us toward a deeper, purer, more meaningful relationship through the powerful magnetism of compatible spirits. Conversely, if we feel uneasy about someone through spiritual discernment, perhaps sensing an arrogant, sinister, or self-centered nature, we are constrained to build a wall and shut that person out.

Spiritual attraction is the first step of the pattern because it's the vital first step toward spiritual communion with God or man. It's the mysterious phenomenon of magnetism between two or more living souls, the draw of the spirit from heart to heart. And while not an action or dynamic in the strictest sense, spiritual attraction is the comforting feeling that starts the journey toward spiritual unity through the heart, the mind, and the soul.

If, however, we reject the call of another's spirit there cannot be a spiritual connection. So if we reject the call of God's Spirit to share his life, we will remain disconnected from him. This is one of the reasons speaking against the Spirit of God will not be forgiven in this world or in the world to come.[144] No one can reject or blaspheme another's spiritual nature and expect to be intimately connected with them. No one! It doesn't work that way.

The Four Colors

In like manner, the four colors of the outer gate were divinely appointed colors that gave testimony to the nature of God's Spirit within. They generated a certain spiritual attraction, because the four colors on the outer gate harmonized with the four colors of the inner veil to create a spiritual attraction to the Spirit within.[145] And although the magnificent colors on outer gate were beautiful in their own right, the true beauty of the gate was not the divinely appointed colors. Its true beauty was the spiritual significance of its colors. Each of its colors revealed a fundamental attribute of the divine nature of God's Holy Spirit within.

Like the spiritual emanations from every living soul that outwardly reveal the fundamental characteristics of their nature within, the four colors of the gate outwardly revealed the fundamental characteristics of God's Spirit within. The four colors on his outer gate and his inner veil were blue, purple, and scarlet threads on finely twined linen (see Exodus 26:31, Exodus 36:35, 37), and each color had a purpose.

> **Blue** signified the universal reign of his Spirit. God is the possessor of heaven and earth. (see Genesis 14:19, 22)
>
> **Purple** signified the supreme royalty of God's Spirit. "I am God almighty." (see Genesis 17:1)
>
> **Scarlet** signified the perfect love of his Spirit, I shed my blood for you. (see Luke 22:20)
>
> **Linen** signified the purity and righteousness of his Spirit. (see 1 John 3:3; Revelation 19:8)

The colors of the outer gate presented a spiritual foretaste of the nature of God's Spirit within, just like the Spirit that rested on Christ presented a spiritual foretaste of God's nature within. As the Son of God, Jesus was God among us, Emmanuel, and by the outward exhibits of his inner nature, he attracted those who hungered and thirsted for the righteousness of God to come and drink his living waters.[146] This is why Jesus could say to Philip, "He that hath seen me hath seen the Father" (John 14:9).

But spiritual attraction is only an invitation, a first step, a point

...spiritual attraction is only an invitation, a first step, a point of beginning. It's the outer gate to the inner soul, but not a completed union.

of beginning. It's the outer gate to the inner soul, but not a completed union.[147] To complete our journey toward spiritual intimacy, we must meet the pattern's requirements to sanctify our hearts for the goal. By

The outreach is his, the response is ours.

God's design, the outer gate for spiritual attraction opens directly into the tabernacle court where the first dynamic of love must be faced for our cleansing. We must be cleansed of all unfaithfulness in the outer court before we can enter the first room of the tabernacle tent—the holy place for spiritual renewal.

We must be called of God before we can respond to his call,[148] and we must draw nigh to God so he will draw nigh to us.[149] The outreach is his, the response is ours. The outer gate is where God's call is made and the court for cleansing is where we perform the first dynamic of agapao love—faithfulness. The author of Hebrews magnified this truth when he told us Jesus went to the *cross* for the *joy* set before him (12:2). The joy set before him was spiritual unity with the Father and us.

...and to come we must respond to his call.

But he that is joined unto the Lord is one spirit. (1 Corinthians 6:17)

In Summary

God's Spirit must draw us before we can come, and to come we must respond to his call. We must follow our forerunner through the pattern's dynamics to sanctify our hearts for the spiritual connection. How else could a pencil pusher like me ever be faultless before the presence of God's glory?

For many are called, but few are chosen.

MATTHEW 22:14

God is faithful, by whom ye were called unto the fellowship
of his Son Jesus Christ our Lord.

1 CORINTHIANS 1:9

Now unto him that is able to keep you from falling,
and to present you faultless before the presence of
his glory with exceeding joy.

JUDE 1:24

Enter ye in at the strait gate: for wide is the gate, and broad is the way,
that leadeth to destruction, and many there be which go in thereat.

MATTHEW 7:13

24

Steps Two and Three: The First Dynamic 🍃

Who shall ascend into the hill of the Lord
or who shall stand in his holy place?
He that hath *clean hands*, and a *pure heart*.

PSALM 24:3-4, ITALICS ADDED

Someone I loved taught me, we are all flawed in one way or another, and because of this, there are three basic categories of people. The first is flawed and doesn't know it. The second is flawed and knows it but does nothing about it. The third is flawed, knows it, and seeks to effect a positive change. I want to be in the third group that seeks to effect a positive change. But sometimes I wonder.

So where do we start? How do we respond to God's call to follow our forerunner and effect a positive change? According to the heavenly pattern, cleansing our hearts of all unrighteousness is how we secure our faithfulness to others. We must dig down to the bedrock of faithfulness to build a stable foundation.

In order to build a sure foundation for any structure, there's no better ground to build on than bedrock. It's usually found under loosely granulated surface materials such as sand, gravel, or soil. To get to the solid rock beneath the surface, the upper layers of these unstable materials must first be removed. So when I found myself in the Rocky

Steps Two and Three: Cleansing the Heart

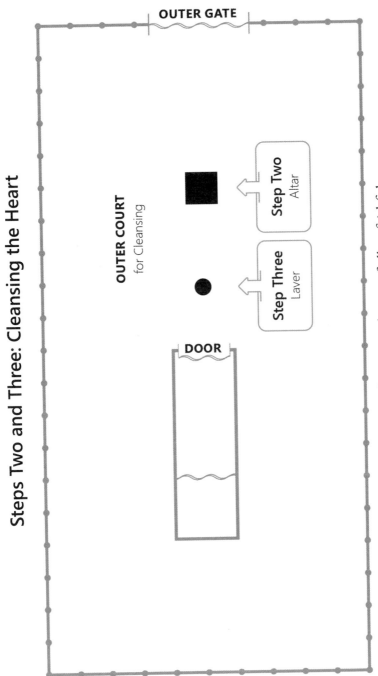

OUTER GATE

OUTER COURT
for Cleansing

DOOR

Step Two
Altar

Step Three
Laver

The first dynamic is to cleanse our hearts of all unfaithfulness.

Mountains because of my desire to remove some unstable materials from my heart and effect a positive change, I became faced with a simple but challenging truth. If I wanted to reconcile my relations with God and others, I needed to build my bridges on the bedrock of faithfulness. But the problem I faced in removing the unstable materials in my heart was that my faithfulness would require my sacrifice. Paul identified these mandatory sacrifices as *putting off the former conduct of the old man* (see Ephesians 4:22).

Spiritual attraction is an invitation, but the faithful performance of love begins with faithfully sacrificing the sins that beset us.[150] Therefore, the stark reality that hit me on that cold October mountain was, *I needed to make a choice.* Would I continue to follow my meandering will and go with the flow to wherever it took me,[151] or would I faithfully give my all in the footsteps of Christ who gave his all to save me?[152] Joshua accepted this challenge of a lifetime when he said, "Choose you this day whom ye will serve…but as for me and my house, we will serve the Lord" (Joshua 24:15). Unlike Joshua, I'd resisted this challenge for so long that to effect the positive change I needed seemed monumental.

> As I considered the strength of their relationship as disclosed in Scripture, it became apparent, if I wanted to be one with them, I needed to become faithful too.

Even the simplest man understands that for any structure to be reliable, its foundation must be built on solid ground. The bridge of hearts is no different. The span of trust between the Father and the Son is built on the solid ground of their faithfulness to each other. Therefore, for any person seeking to enter their trust and become one with them must effect a positive change. As I considered the strength of their relationship as disclosed in Scripture, it became apparent, if

I wanted to be one with them, I needed to become faithful too (see Galatians 3:9). I needed to face this monumental challenge.

I will even betroth thee unto me in faithfulness: and thou shalt know the Lord. (Hosea 2:20)

A sacrifice is an act of faithfulness based on a belief or hope that the result will be better. The decision to make a personal sacrifice becomes a faithful act when we give up something we hold dear in the hopes of replacing it with something more precious. Jesus demonstrated this truth in Gethsemane when he said, "Not my will, but thine" (Luke 22:42). Then he yielded his will to the Father's and endured the cross of Calvary for something he considered more precious—us.

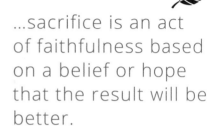

...sacrifice is an act of faithfulness based on a belief or hope that the result will be better.

Who died for us, that, whether we wake or sleep, we should live together with him. (1 Thessalonians 5:10)

Step Two: The Altar Is for Sacrifice

I beseech you therefore, brethren, by the mercies of God, that ye present your bodies a living sacrifice, holy, acceptable unto God, which is your reasonable service. (Romans 12:1)

Looking back to the Day of Atonement in ancient Israel, when the high priest entered the outer court of the tabernacle, he was faced with two implements for cleansing: the altar for sacrifice and the laver for washing. The altar stood in the front and center of the court near the outer gate, so it could not be ignored, overlooked, or willingly bypassed. Beyond the altar, the laver stood for examining his heart in the basin's mirrors and for washing his hands and feet in the water.[153] The forward placement of the altar and laver in the outer court signified that the priest had to be fully cleansed before entering the tabernacle tent.

Nobody likes the altar. Why should we? Personal sacrifice goes against every grain of our natural instinct to protect and preserve our two most cherished possessions—our lives and our will. The ominous fires of the altar threaten and intimidate us

...placing our all on the altar is how we pull the bad weeds so we can plant the good seeds.

with the fear of dying to self. But placing our *all* on the altar is how we pull the bad weeds so we can plant the good seeds.

I once perceived the altar as a lethal threat, a dreaded end. The truth, however, is quite the opposite. The altar is the place for new beginnings. It's where Christ gave his life for ours so we might have life with him, and it's the way we must go if we want to follow his lead to find new life in God. Sure, the altar brings death to our former way of thinking and living, but if we follow our forerunner's lead and face the altar's fire, we will find the altar is life giving. It is where our love for our failing old nature will be replaced with a love for God's ever-increasing new nature so we can return God's standard of love. Good trade!

The altar is the place for new beginnings.

And walk in love, as Christ also has loved us and has given Himself for us, an offering and a sacrifice to God for a sweet-smelling aroma. (Ephesians 5:2, NKJV)

Step Three: Washing in the Waters of the Laver

That he might sanctify and cleanse it with the washing of water by the word. (Ephesians 5:26)

The laver for washing was the next step for cleansing, it was the designated fixture for washing, while sanctifying the priest's heart in the waters of God's word.[154] The laver was the second step for cleansing and the third step of the pattern. It, too, was in the outer court, between the altar and the tabernacle tent, where the priest could examine his heart in its mirrored basin while washing his hands and feet. The laver had a brass bowl about waist high, made from the polished mirrors of the women,[155] and a second basin at its base, called a foot, for washing his feet.[156] The priest would peer into the mirrors through the water in the bowl to examine his heart for anything unclean while washing in the water.

The act of cleansing the whole man through blood and water was symbolic of being washed in the blood of God's Lamb[157] and the waters of God's word.[158] John must have been thinking about this sacrament of washing when he wrote, "Sanctify them through thy truth: thy word is truth" (17:17).

As it was with the priest, placing our sacrifices on the altar and then reflecting on God's word to finish cleansing our hearts is how it works—how we repent—how we begin to effect a positive change. Following Christ through this cleansing process makes the distinction between religious talk and relational walk, and that subtle distinction makes all the difference in the world when it comes to the joy of the unity—it's how we clean our closets.

> Following Christ through this cleansing process makes the distinction between religious talk and relational walk.

The psalmist told us God knows the secrets of the heart (see Psalm 44:21, NASB). Since God knows the secrets of our hearts, then we are all transparent before him, like it or not. Our Creator who knows everything about us, secrets and all, says if we want to be one with him in the freedom of a holy and unblemished union, *we must come clean*—our skeletons must go.

Thou blind Pharisee, cleanse first that which is within the cup and platter, that the outside of them may be clean also. (Matthew 23:26)

Entering the Tent

Once the requirements for cleansing were met in the court, the priest was prepared to enter the tabernacle tent for the second dynamic of the pattern—the renewal of a right spirit. Renewal takes place in the first room of the tabernacle tent called the holy place. It's where we spark the light of God's Spirit in our hearts to form Christ within us.

The same beautiful person who taught me about the three basic categories of people also taught me, "We plant our own garden." We must cleanse our hearts and then implant our hearts with the right seed for the right spirit. According to Scripture, the right seed is God's word of truth[159] and the right spirit is God's Holy Spirit. Cleansing our heart is how we weed our garden, and sowing God's word is how we plant our garden. Cleansing the heart prepares the soil, but we are not a finished work until the seed of God's Spirit matures within us and we bare the fruit of God's Spirit to the husbandman of the vineyard.

But the fruit of the Spirit is love, joy, peace, longsuffering,

> "We plant our own garden."

> Cleansing our heart is how we weed our garden, and sowing God's word is how we plant our garden.

gentleness, goodness, faith, meekness, temperance: against such there is no law. (Galatians 5:22–23)

Unto him that loved us and washed us from our sins in his own blood.

REVELATION 1:5

Not by works of righteousness which we have done, but according to his mercy he saved us, by the washing of regeneration [*in the court of cleansing*], and renewing of the Holy Ghost [*in the holy place*].

TITUS 3:5

Now ye are clean through the word which I have spoken unto you.

JOHN 15:3

Behold, the husbandman waiteth for the precious fruit of the earth.

JAMES 5:7

And other [seed] fell on good ground, and sprang up, and bare fruit an hundredfold.

LUKE 8:8

25

Steps Four and Five: The Second Dynamic 🌿

Behold, thou desirest truth in the inward parts: and in the hidden part thou shalt make me to know wisdom.

PSALM 51:6

I grew up in Jacksonville, Florida, a beautiful coastal city divided east to west and north to south by the stately St. Johns River. Three of the bridges crossing the river have been replaced since I was a boy, a fourth remains in good repair, while a fifth, the Dames Point Bridge, was built after I became a man. All five of these bridges have a variety of structural characteristics in common, one of the most important being their supporting pillars. Although varied by design, each bridge has solid structural pillars grounded deep in the bed of the river to provide reliable supports for their connecting spans.

In the natural world we live in, every connecting span across any gulf or river must have solid structural pillars to survive the challenges of time. The bridge of hearts is no different. To remain eternally reliable, the span of trust must be firmly upheld with reliable structural pillars that stand on the solid rock bedrock of faithfulness. According to the Holy Scripture, there are seven of these pillars that uphold our spiritual connections—seven pillars of truth that are in the hearts of the Father and the Son—the seven Spirits of God.

Steps Four and Five: Renewing the Heart

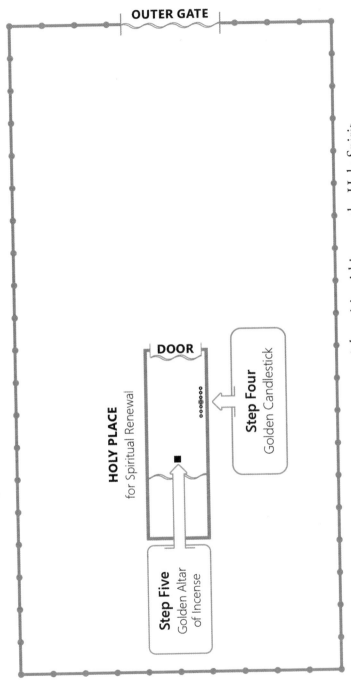

OUTER GATE

HOLY PLACE
for Spiritual Renewal

DOOR

Step Four
Golden Candlestick

Step Five
Golden Altar
of Incense

The second dynamic is to renew a right spirit within us—the Holy Spirit.

Referring to God

Seven lamps of fire were burning before the throne, which are *the seven Spirits of God.* (Revelation 4:5, NKJV, italics added)

Referring to Christ

And unto the angel of the church in Sardis write; These things saith he [Jesus] *that hath the seven Spirits of God.* (Revelation 3:1, italics added)

That God's Holy Spirit has seven spiritual pillars is clearly seen in Revelation 1:4, 4:5, and 5:6. And according to Revelation 3:1 and 5:6, Jesus, God's first begotten Son, has been given God's seven Spirits too. And because God's nature is truth, I must conclude his seven Spirits are pillars of truth. John wrote God's "word is truth" (17:17) and his Spirit is truth (see John 14:17), The Psalmist wrote he is the "God of truth" (Psalm 31:5), his "commandments are truth" (Psalm 119:151), and he desires truth in our inward parts (see Psalm 51:6). Then James confirmed that God is begetting "us with the word of truth" (1:18). So I must conclude, the seven Spirits of God that sustain his nature with love are pillars of spiritual truth. Therefore, it is also reasonable to surmise these seven pillars of divine truth must be formed in our hearts as well to make us compatible with the Father and the Son.

Lord, who shall abide in thy tabernacle? Who shall dwell in thy holy hill? He that walketh uprightly, and worketh righteousness, and *speaketh the truth in his heart.* (Psalm 15:1–2 italics added)

We are designed for the habitation of God through the Spirit who reveals, nurtures, and develops his truth within us.[160] So if the Spirit of God is born in the good soil of a good heart, we are going to continue to grow and change until we bear fruit. Our hearts will be steadily renewed and increased through the development of God's Spirit until we become mature in the stature and fullness of Christ. In the parable of the sower, Jesus spoke of this growing process when he said that his seed brought forth *fruit with patience.*[161]

David's Witness

David spoke of the pattern's first and second dynamics for spiritual cleansing and renewal when he prayed, "Create in me a *clean heart*, O God; and renew a *right spirit* within me" (Psalm 51:10, italics added). David's prayer was in harmony with the protocol of the pattern, first cleansing and then renewal. His prayer had everything to do with wanting to be cleansed from his transgressions and having the right spirit renewed in his heart so he would be acceptable to God. David understood the protocol of the pattern so well that he used his knowledge of the pattern to design Solomon's temple (see 1 Chronicles 28:11–21). David also wrote, "Who shall ascend into the hill of the Lord? or who shall stand in his holy place? He that hath clean hands, and a pure heart" (Psalm 24:3–4).

> David's prayer was in harmony with the protocol of the pattern, first cleansing and then renewal.

The Tabernacle Tent

After having been cleansed at the altar and laver in the outer court, the high priest would leave the court by stepping through the door to the first room of the tabernacle tent. The rectangular tent had two rooms that were divided by a curtain called the inner veil. The first room was called the holy place and the second room, the holiest place. The holy place is where the golden candlestick stood with its seven lamps, which represented the seven Spirits of God that are burning before his throne (see Revelation 4:5). The priest had to light the seven lamps with coals from his sacrifice at the altar before he could proceed as seen below.

And he shall take a censer full of *burning coals of fire from off the altar* before the Lord, and his hands full of sweet incense beaten small, and bring it within the vail. (Leviticus 16:12, italics added)

Step Four: Lighting the Golden Candlestick

Lighting the seven lamps was step four. The golden candlestick was an olive oil candelabra: a gold fixture featuring a center column with a lamp on its top and six branches with the same lamps on their tops. The six branches on their tops. The six branches extended from the center column. There were three branches on the left side of the column and three on the right side making a total of seven lamps in all. If you've ever seen a menorah with seven lamps, you've seen a replica of the golden candlestick.

without sacrifice there would be no spiritual light.

Lighting these lamps required a sacrifice in the outer court first, because according to the above passage from Leviticus, God required the priest to use coals from the sacrifice on the altar to light the seven lamps. *No other fire could be used*; therefore, without sacrifice there would be no spiritual light.

Lighting the seven lamps was symbolic of kindling the light of life in our hearts—God's Spirit. Paul referred to this process of spiritual renewal as forming Christ within us.[162] I think of it as *lighting our eternal flames*, of transforming us from our first order of mortal beings—the natural offspring of man, into the last order of immortal beings—the spiritual offspring of God. We must be cleansed through sacrifice at the altar to have the light of God's Spirit kindled within us, and his Spirit must be kindled within us to have his light of life.

I am the light of the world: he that followeth me shall not walk in darkness, but *shall have the light of life.* (John 8:12, italics added)

Step Five: The Golden Altar of Incense

Another angel came and stood at the altar, holding a golden censer; and much incense was given to him, so that he might add it to the prayers of all the saints on the golden altar which was before the throne. *And the smoke of the incense, with the prayers of the saints, went up before God out of the angel's hand.* (Revelation 8:3–4, NASB, italics added)

The golden altar of incense is where prayerful petitions were made by the priest for their acceptance beyond the veil. Petitioning another's heart for forgiveness and acceptance is an appeal, not a right. Reconciliation is not something we can demand even if we give our lives to be burned (see 1 Corinthians 13:3). The choice to forgive and accept is the right of the person petitioned—not the petitioner. No one is duty-bound to break down his or her wall and extend grace just because the request is made—especially not God. If the person who is being petitioned believes that caution is in order, their freedom of choice must be respected.

> I think of it as *lighting our eternal flames...*

The golden altar of incense stood in the holy place, against the outside of the veil protecting God's holiest place, which is the same veil that divided the

> Reconciliation is not something we can demand even if we give our lives to be burned (see 1 Corinthians 13:3).

tabernacle tent into two separate rooms. The prayers of the priest were accompanied by incense to put a sweet-smelling fragrance in prayerful petitions. This incense was also lit by the coals from the sacrifice on the altar. Once the priest lit the incense with coals from the sacrifice, the fragrant smoke would ascend beyond the veil to the mercy seat, where the Spirit of God was visibly enthroned.[163] Hence, without sacrifice, there is no sweet-smelling fragrance in prayer.

> Incense represents the sweet spiritual fragrance of a cleansed and renewed heart in the prayerful petitions of the priest.

The same King David who prayed for cleansing and renewal of a right spirit in his heart also prayed, "Let my prayer be set before Thee as incense" (Psalm 141:2). Incense represents the sweet spiritual fragrance of a cleansed and renewed heart in the prayerful petitions of the priest. It's like the fragrant petition the woman made when she broke the alabaster box, and the fragrant petition Jesus would make when asking the Father to remove his veil.

> The Levitical high priest who foreshadowed Christ offered restitution for the sins of the nation, but the true last High Priest, Jesus the Christ, offered restitution for the sins of the world.

Just as the Levite priest's petitions had to be heard and accepted before he could enter beyond the veil to render the blood of his sacrifice for sin, the petitions of Christ had to be heard and accepted before he could enter beyond the veil to render the same. The Levitical high priest who foreshadowed Christ offered restitution for the sins of the nation, but the true last High Priest, Jesus the Christ, offered restitution for the sins of the world. This is why God ripped his veil to receive the blood of Christ.

Jesus surrendered his life's blood on and before God's mercy seat as the propitiation for the sins of the world. Then God accepted his blood atonement for our cleansing and established the new covenant of grace for our eternal salvation. After having blotted out the many ordinances against us, God the Father seated Jesus the Son at his own right hand as our advocate,[164] mediator,[165] and true high priest of our profession.[166] Jesus could then shepherd our walk through the pattern's three dynamics.[167]

But this man [Jesus], after he had offered one sacrifice for sins forever, sat down on the right hand of God. (Hebrews 10:12)

Which vail is done away in Christ.

2 CORINTHIANS 3:14

Neither by the blood of goats and calves, but by his own blood he entered in once into the holy place, having *obtained eternal redemption for us.*

HEBREW 9:12, ITALICS ADDED

Not by works of righteousness which we have done, but according to his mercy he saved us, by the washing of regeneration [cleansing], and renewing of the Holy Ghost [spiritual renewal]; Which he shed on us abundantly through Jesus Christ our Saviour.

TITUS 3:5

Whereby are given unto us exceeding great and precious promises: that by these ye might be partakers of the divine nature.

2 PETER 1:4

26

Steps Six and Seven: The Third Dynamic 🖋

Draw nigh to God, and he will draw nigh to you.

JAMES 4:8

The monsoons in Vietnam seem to last forever if you live in the bush with only a poncho to sleep in. During the worst part of those rain-filled months of 1969, supplies were difficult to helicopter into the high hills due to the frequent downpours and misty fog, so we sometimes went hungry for days. Additionally, our bodies became pickled by weeks of wet clothing. We couldn't change our clothes; we had nothing to change into. I often wondered if our enemy could smell the layers of our dead and waterlogged skin while we were on our nightly ambushes.

One evening at dusk while five of us were setting up an L-shaped ambush in the fading light and drizzle of rain, the closing darkness reduced our visibility so terribly we could barely see our silhouettes. It was then we realized there was a sixth man among us. Apparently, he'd thought we were some of his comrades and was just as confused as we were. Quickly squatting in the waist-high grass, none of us knew how many more might be with him or if they were about to hit us as the blanket of nightfall absorbed our silhouettes in its murky shadows.

Steps Six and Seven: Surrendering the Heart

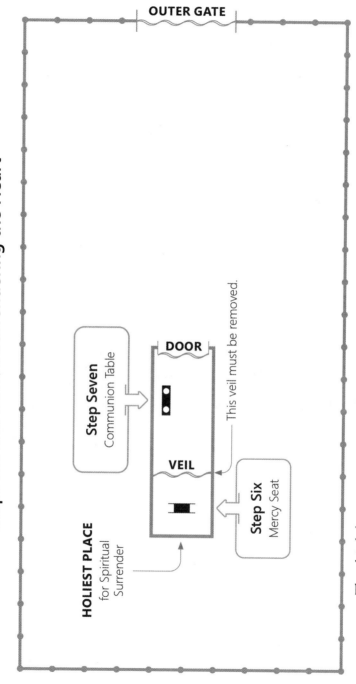

OUTER GATE

Step Seven
Communion Table

DOOR

VEIL

This veil must be removed.

Step Six
Mercy Seat

HOLIEST PLACE
for Spiritual Surrender

The third dynamic is to surrender a humble and contrite heart to God or others.

Shattering the quiet, the man called out in his Vietnamese tongue. Our hearts were pounding. Judging by the sound of his voice, he had crawled no more than thirty to forty feet away from where we sat frozen in the silence of time.

Being the M60 machine gunner, I always carried a .45 caliber pistol on my hip in case my machine gun jammed, so our squad leader whispered for me to crawl out and shoot him with my pistol. It is easier to crawl with a ready pistol than a ready rifle. Thankfully, he also sent a rifleman to tail me.

When we couldn't find the man in the dark, I turned to the rifleman and whispered for him to crawl back and have them shoot up a flare, which we called a pop-up. I knew the man we hunted was very close, and with a little light I might be luckier than him. As the rifleman crawled away, I was left alone in the unnerving darkness.

Lying quietly on the ground, the sound of my beating heart muffled the sound of the rain pelting my helmet and steadily pouring down my nose and chin. Time stood still. It seemed an eternity passed before the rifleman returned with new orders. We crawled back to the others without shooting a pop-up, or the man. Our squad leader had wisely chosen not to give the ghost in the darkness our exact position.

We then moved a couple of hundred yards down the trail and sat on full alert all night in the rain, not knowing how many more soldiers might be lurking in the shadows and planning to hit us hard. We couldn't accurately assess our situation until the gray haze of misty dawn began to reveal the large stands of tall bamboo dotting the grassy expanse. As we started packing our gear and breaking out of the ambush, I noticed what seemed to be a man's face obscured in one of the bamboo clusters about fifty yards away. Leaving the machine gun in place, I picked up my assistant gunner's rifle and diagonally approached the thick stand of bamboo while keeping the ambiguous face in the corner of my eye. He ran. The rapid crack of the M16 sent three rounds in the blur of a moment. He cartwheeled.

I'd hunted deer when I was a boy and I knew how to track a wounded animal—one spot of blood at a time. But while focused on tracking, I became separated from the others and eventually came alone to a fork in the faint traces of the grassy trail. While looking hard for the next spot of blood to determine which direction the man had gone, my heart leaped through my spine when he cried out with hysterical sobs at no more than five feet from where I stood.

Having crawled into a hole, he'd pulled the grass down over him to hide his wounded body. Failing to notice the distortion in the grass could easily have resulted in a fatal mistake. At five feet or less, any man with a pistol could've easily shot me, but he chose to surrender his life instead. In his desperate situation, where nothing was certain, he chose rightly. He chose life over death when he made the tough decision to surrender his all and trust me.

Holding the muzzle of the rifle hard against his chest, I removed the Russian-made pistol from his belt and called to the others. It wasn't until after they'd helicoptered him out of the bush to an American hospital in Da Nang that reality hit me. His total surrender probably saved my life too.

I have told this story because total surrender is what this chapter is all about. Total surrender is to yield completely to the power or control of another's compulsion or demand. It's to give oneself as a prisoner, bondservant, or slave through voluntary or involuntary means.

> So surrender should be seriously considered by those who want to live.

Most of the authors of the New Testament, including Paul, Peter, John, James, and Jude, use the Greek word *doulos* ("bondman, servant, or slave") to describe their voluntary surrender to Christ and to one another. They chose rightly, they chose life over death when they made the tough decision to surrender their all and trust Christ.

Even though there's a big difference between those bondservants of Christ, who surrendered their lives out of a voluntary love, and the Vietnamese officer, who surrendered his life out of an involuntary fear, both surrendered their lives with hope, and both found the life they hoped for. So surrender should be seriously considered by those who want to live. Jesus said, "And whosoever will be chief

We were also built to give love.

among you, let him be your servant [doulos]: Even as the Son of man came not to be ministered unto, but to minister, and to give his life a ransom for many" (Matthew 20:28). Then he led our way through the pattern's dynamics and surrendered his life for ours.[168]

I lay down my life for the sheep. (John 10:15)

We were not built to just receive love, hoard it, self-direct it, or amass great quantities of the love from others in a stagnant heart. We were also built to give love.[169] God's love must flow into our hearts and out of our bellies as rivers of living water,[170] or we will stagnate within and die. This helps me to understand why the surrender of a contrite heart is such a desirable sacrifice to God.[171] A truly surrendered heart is a faithful heart that lays down its life for others.

Greater love hath no man than this, that a man lay down his life for his friends. (John 15:13)

The kind of surrender God calls for is not about being bound to a strict set of legal or religious traditions. Those religious works

God has surrendered his heart to ours through his one offering for sin, now the onus is on us to surrender our hearts to his and consummate the cycle.

merely dominate people's lives with man-made ordinances such as "touch not; taste not; handle not" (Colossians 2:21). Nor is surrender about extraordinary deeds like giving our bodies to be burned, although many have been martyred because they were faithful to love him. It's about yielding our will to God's will and then following our forerunner through the narrow way of the pattern to surrender our life to God's.[172] This kind of love fulfills the whole law of love.[173]

And though I bestow all my goods to feed the poor, and though I give my body to be burned, and have not charity, *it profiteth me nothing.* (1 Corinthians 13:3, italics added)

> ## God's mercy seat is the most applauded place in the whole realm of creation.

In our sphere of spiritual emotions, voluntarily surrendering our hearts to God or man has everything to do with placing our trust in the one we are surrendering to. And, of course, when total surrender is freely exchanged between two hearts, the span of trust is firmly fixed and the cycle of life becomes timeless. In our world today, God has surrendered his heart to ours through his one offering for sin, now the onus is on us to surrender our hearts to his and consummate the cycle.

As for God…*he is a buckler to all those that trust in him.* (Psalm 18:30, italics added)

Step Six: Surrendering at the Mercy Seat

And there will I meet with thee, and I will commune with thee from above the mercy seat. (Exodus 25:22)

God's mercy seat is where it's at. It is where the New Testament covenant was established, where Jesus surrendered his life to God, and where God extended his mercy to us. It's where the blood of

God's Lamb was sprinkled and the gift of God's clemency was granted—where grace was extended and reconciliation was made through the powerful exchange of unblemished love from two unblemished hearts—the Father's and the Son's. It is the sixth step of the pattern where the one sacrifice for our sin was given to cleanse and justify us, where the joy of our salvation was born.

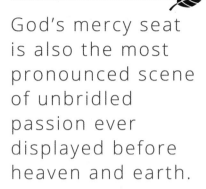

God's mercy seat is also the most pronounced scene of unbridled passion ever displayed before heaven and earth.

Behold, God is my salvation; I will trust, and not be afraid: for the Lord Jehovah is my strength and my song; he also is become my salvation. (Isaiah 12:2)

God's mercy seat is the most applauded place in the whole realm of creation. It's where the greatest covenant of all was confirmed between our Creator God and his created people. In this holiest place of God where his Spirit sits enthroned on mercy, the new covenant of grace was sealed with the blood of Christ, to secure our rite of passage into God's eternal kingdom.

Once the veil was removed, all of creation could see and rejoice that God's Spirit was enthroned on mercy.

God's mercy seat is also the most pronounced scene of unbridled passion ever displayed before heaven and earth. So great was our Father's emotional release when Jesus surrendered his blood surety for the new covenant that God ripped his veil from top to bottom with the fervent passion of a father's love to receive his first begotten Son,[174] our forerunner—the firstfruits of the resurrection.

> But every man in his own order: Christ the firstfruits; afterward they that are Christ's at his coming. (1 Corinthians 15:23)

Once the veil was removed, all of creation could see and rejoice that God's Spirit was enthroned on mercy. This beautiful portrayal of God's passion for mercy is the substance of our hope in God's clemency. Mercy is the higher part of the law; the capstone of our redemption, which is why God's Spirit was seated on mercy above the testimony law that was placed in the ark.[175] James told us "mercy rejoiceth against judgment" (2:13), and this is what mercy will always do, because mercy is the compassionate part of the law that allows for a guilty person's return to innocence—for a new beginning through the unmerited favor of grace.

"mercy rejoiceth against judgment"

But the mercy seat would remain isolated in the second room, behind the veil, until Christ made restitution for all men and our God could remove his veil to expose his heart.

> It is of the Lord's mercies that we are not consumed, because his compassions fail not. They are new every morning: great is thy faithfulness. (Lamentations 3:22–23)

Before the veil was torn,[176] the last room of the tabernacle tent, the holiest place, contained only one fixture—the mercy seat above the ark where God's Spirit was visibly enthroned.[177] The other fixtures of the tabernacle were in the first room of the tent called the holy place.

These fixtures were the golden candlestick, the altar of incense, and the communion table. But the mercy seat would remain isolated in the second room, behind the veil, until Christ made restitution for all men and our God could remove his veil to expose his heart.

The mercy seat was the lid for the ark of the covenant. Beneath the mercy seat, the ark contained God's testimony of law. God's mercy seat was above the tablets of law for a predetermined purpose that should never go unnoticed—its higher position testified of the preeminence of mercy over judgment.[178]

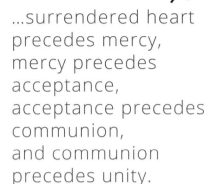

...surrendered heart precedes mercy, mercy precedes acceptance, acceptance precedes communion, and communion precedes unity.

The apostle James clearly told us, "Mercy rejoiceth against judgment" (2:13), Paul told us that God is rich in mercy (see Ephesians 2:4), and David wrote, "O give thanks unto the Lord, for he is good: for his mercy endureth forever" (Psalms 107:1). God proved how great his mercy is when he replaced the old covenant of law that no man could keep, with the new covenant of grace that no man could earn, by sending his darling to die for us, so that he could remove his veil and receive those who followed as one of his greatly beloved.[179]

This is why total surrender is the choice we must make if total acceptance is the prize that we seek.

One of the greatest truths I have learned on my earthly trek is, a surrendered heart precedes mercy, mercy precedes acceptance, acceptance precedes communion, and communion precedes unity. Surrendering the heart is the third dynamic of the pattern because a surrendered heart is a trustworthy heart, and, of course, a trustworthy heart is a heart that has consigned itself to be faithful and true. This is why total surrender is the choice we must make if total acceptance is the prize that we seek.[180] Jesus confirmed this principle before heaven and earth when he surrendered his life to God on his mercy seat to gain his Father's sanction for our acceptance in the beloved.

Much like the Vietnamese officer, we don't have any hope for life unless we surrender our lives to the One who holds our future. Jesus told us, "He that findeth his life shall lose it: and he that loseth his life for my sake shall find it" (Matthew 10:39), then he said, "take up your cross and follow me." Jesus knew God's love was larger than life and that his mercy rejoiced against judgment, which is why he called us to *follow him.*

In whom we have redemption through his blood, the forgiveness of sins, according to the riches of his grace. (Ephesians 1:7)

Step Seven: The Communion Table

That ye may eat and drink at my table in my kingdom. (Luke 22:30)

Breaking bread at God's communion table is the seventh and final step of the pattern, the prize we seek. The name *shewbread* means "the bread of faces" or "the bread of presence," meaning the presence of God is face to face with the presence of man.[181] I cannot imagine the joy that day will hold for God the Father and for those he has called to be glorified with Christ.

Jesus is the first and only man ever laden with all the sins of the world and the first and only man to follow the pattern's protocol for radical reconciliation. Therefore, he was the first man to see the veil fall,[182] and the first Son of man to be seated at God's table of honor for face-to-face communion. Among the many great things Jesus was sent to do for us, removing the veil to connect our hearts was clearly his highest priority. God's wall had to fall for the bridge of hearts to be built, and the bridge had to be built for us to be one with him.

Before the veil was torn, the communion table stood in the first room of the tent called the holy place, it was never in the holiest place. The table was in front of the veil, and there is no known record that God was ever seated with any man at his communion table while it remained on the outside of the veil. There couldn't be face-to-face communion between God and man until man was cleansed of all unrighteousness and renewed with the right Spirit, because no natural, carnal man could see God's face and live.

> God's wall had to fall for the bridge of hearts to be built, and the bridge had to be built for us to be one with him.

One Room

God's Spirit had remained behind the veil in his holiest place maintaining a separation from all men until Christ fulfilled the law of love for us so God could remove his veil. *What is extremely important to notice is,* once Christ's mission was accomplished and the veil was torn, *the holy place and the holiest place became one room.* The two rooms became one large room, no longer curtained by a veil. The room outside of the veil, the holy place for phileo love, became one with the room on the inside of the veil, God's holiest place for agapao love. Then the communion table with its bread of faces was in the same room with God and man, and it became the center of the action.

> The two rooms became one large room, no longer curtained by a veil.

The newly conjoined room was all-inclusive. Once the veil was done away with, the one room contained all seven of the fixtures in the tabernacle tent. It had the light of God's Spirit from the golden candlestick, the passionate fragrance of a pure and contrite heart from the altar of incense, the ark of God's covenant where his mercy was enthroned over the tablets of law, and the communion table with its bread of faces and communion wine.

God's grant of clemency holds no bounds.

> But I say unto you, I will not drink henceforth of this fruit of the vine, until that day when I drink it new with you in my Father's kingdom. (Matthew 26:29)

The Invitation

The invitation to God's banquet table is unrivaled by any other invitation in the history of creation, and it has been extended to every man, woman, and child, whether common or great or rich or poor. Everyone has been invited to come to the table of God, because God's grant of clemency holds no bounds.

...they long for a chair at his table of honor to share the bread of faces.

Those who are invited to God's table of honor are not some exclusive sect of religious elite or educated nobility who think they have no need for a physician.[183] The Spirit calls all men, saying, "Whosoever will, let him take the water of life freely" (Revelation 22:17).[184] "Whosoever will" includes everyone who is hungry and thirsty for righteousness: Even people like myself who have demanded their way more times than they can count and are thirsty for the righteousness of God.[185] The Spirit's call is to anyone and everyone who will surrender their hearts to God, because they long for a chair at his table of honor to share the bread of faces.

And they shall come from the east, and from the west, and from the north, and from the south, and shall sit down in the kingdom of God. (Luke 13:29)

Blessed is he that shall eat bread in the kingdom of God. (Luke 14:15)

...which is why his ultimate objective for us was to bring us face to face with the Father, under the covenant of grace, so we could share the bread of faces.

In Summary

Jesus's journey to God's holiest place began in Gethsemane where he yielded his will to God's. It was then culminated after he surrendered his all to the mercy seat of God in the heavens. In between Gethsemane and heaven, Jesus endured the cross for his cleansing and he was renewed with the seven Spirits of God (Revelation 3:1, 5:6).

...he proved the dynamics of the pattern were eternally reliable.

As the forerunner and shepherd of all who would follow his lead, Jesus paved our way to an intimate connection with God that no man had known before—no man. In so doing, he proved the dynamics of the pattern were eternally reliable. Then, after reconciling us to God by meeting the pattern's requirements, he was exalted to the Father's right hand where he champions our cause as our faithful High Priest, advocate, mediator, and intercessor.[186] Jesus's whole objective was and is to please the Father,[187] which is why his ultimate objective for us was to bring us face to face with the Father, under the covenant of grace, so we could share the bread of faces.

Jesus called us to follow him, and then he led our way through the narrow way that leads to life—the way of the pattern—the way of the Via Dolorosa. I am convinced by my seventy trips around the sun that any person who rejects God's spiritual instructions for following his Son will never soar to the high and lofty places of the One who inhabits eternity. But if we choose to follow our forerunner through these life-changing dynamics that God has given for our instruction, we will rise from the dust in glorious bodies to finish our course with joy.

Who shall change our vile body, that it may be fashioned like unto his glorious body. (Philippians 3:21)

Neither count I my life dear unto myself, so that I might
finish my course with joy.

ACTS 20:24, ITALICS ADDED

Not that I have already obtained all this, or have already
arrived at my goal, but I press on to take hold of that for which
Christ Jesus took hold of me.

PHILIPPIANS 3:12, NIV

I have fought a good fight, *I have finished my course*, I have kept the
faith: Henceforth there is laid up for me a crown of righteousness.

2 TIMOTHY 4:7–8, ITALICS ADDED

How shall we escape, if we neglect so great a salvation?

HEBREWS 2:3, NKJV

27

The Seven Spirits of God 🌿

Seven lamps of fire were burning before the throne, which are *the seven Spirits of God.*

REVELATION 4:5, NKJV, ITALICS ADDED

P eople speculate and develop theories about many things. Out of these theories come the world of science where we seek to discover the truth. The increase in our scientific pursuits has increased our knowledge and improved our quality of life in many ways. So, in like manner, I think it would be good to speculate and develop theories about the seven Spirits of God. I believe an investigation of his seven Spirits will improve our knowledge of him and increase our quality of life.

I will readily admit that I can't confirm the identities of God's seven Spirits beyond a reasonable doubt, so I've debated about including this somewhat speculative chapter. The reason there are speculations and theories about the identities of these seven Spirits' is they're not clearly identified in Scripture, so proving their identities is not so easily done—perhaps not possible in this present world. But following the advice in Proverbs has inspired my ongoing search. Solomon wrote, "It is the glory of God to conceal a thing: but the honor of kings is to search out a matter" (25:2). So I began to search them out.

To begin with, I suspect the seven Spirits of God are one and the same with the seven pillars of wisdom. Solomon wrote, "Wisdom hath builded her house, she hath hewn out her seven pillars" (Proverbs 9:1), then John told us God has seven Spirits, and Paul said we are the house of God. So it all seems to connect. If the seven pillars of wisdom are one and the same with the seven Spirits of God, then to become a member of God's household,[188] we must have these seven pillars formed in our hearts as well.

> Ye also, as lively stones, are built up a spiritual house. (1 Peter 2:5)

...our house must be built on God's truth to be built with God's wisdom.

Solomon taught us that acquiring wisdom is the principal thing, saying, if you get her, you get understanding, and understanding brings honor (see Proverbs 4:4–9); James told us to receive God's implanted word that is able to save our souls; and Peter told us we must become partakers of the divine nature. So to get true wisdom, we must implant God's word of truth in our hearts, because, wisdom and truth are sisters[189]—we can't have wisdom without it. Therefore, our house must be built on God's truth to be built with God's wisdom.

> Whosoever *heareth these sayings of mine, and doeth them*, I will liken him unto a wise man, which built his house upon a rock. (Matthew 7:24, italics added)

As we have repeatedly seen in previous chapters, God's word of truth is the seed of his Spirit. Just as it is best to sow good seed in good soil, God's seed must be implanted in the good soil of an honest and good heart to reproduce God's nature within it.[190] This new life in the heart is what Paul called the earnest of the Spirit.[191] But like any seed, once it germinates it still takes time to mature and bear fruit.[192] Again, Jesus validated this growing process in the parable

> This new life in the heart is what Paul called the earnest of the Spirit.

of the sower when he said, "But that on the good ground are they, which in *an honest and good heart*, having heard the word, keep it, and *bring forth fruit with patience*" (Luke 8:15, italics added). Then James wrote, "Let patience have its perfect work" (1:4). So patience has a key role in our spiritual development.

In the natural world, a seed that's sown in good soil reproduces the shoot, then the branches, and then the natural fruit. Likewise, in the spiritual world, a seed that's sown in good soil reproduces the shoot, then the branches, and then the spiritual fruit.

> When God's Spirit is born within us, the first shoot out of God's seed is his *Spirit of life*—the earnest of the Spirit.

When God's Spirit is born within us, the first shoot out of God's seed is his *Spirit of life*— the earnest of the Spirit. Once his Spirit of life is born within us it then branches out with the other six Spirits to bear the fruit of the Spirit to the husbandman of the vineyard. The menorah, with its main candlestick and six branches, gives a natural illustration of this light of God's life within us.

Then spake Jesus again unto them, saying, I am the light of the world: he that followeth me shall not walk in darkness, *but shall have the light of life*. (John 8:12, italics added)

In searching Scripture for the identities of these seven Spirits, I've drawn some conclusions I believe have merit. There are several all-inclusive names or designations for God's Holy Spirit, such as the *Spirit of the Lord* and the *Spirit of God*, but these don't identify the seven facets of God's Spirit. I have also considered the prophet Isaiah's mention of the six spirits of the Lord that rested on Christ (see 11:1–2), but *I have rejected this option for three reasons.* First, there are only six spirits in Isaiah's prophecy, not seven; second, the six spirits rested on Christ, not in him; and third, the fear of the Lord [yhwh] is one of the six spirits Isaiah listed that would rest on Christ. The fear of the Lord did rest on Christ beyond all doubt, but it could not be one of God's seven Spirits because God does not fear himself. Therefore, I must conclude, Isaiah's prophecy could not have been given to identify the seven Spirits of God, and this is good cause for further research.

> The fear of the Lord did rest on Christ beyond all doubt, but it could not be one of God's seven Spirits because God does not fear himself.

There are, however, seven Spirits recorded in the New Testament that do name and identify seven facets of God's Spirit that are in the heart of the Father and the Son. As I've reflected on the development of these seven Spirits within us, I've put a sequence to their development that appears reasonable. The sequence begins with the birth of God's Spirit of life in our hearts and ends with the finishing touches of his Spirit of glory resting on us.

1. *Spirit of life* (see Romans 8:2): God's seed reproduces the earnest of his Spirit within us (see 2 Corinthians 1:22, 5:5).

2. *Spirit of truth* (see John 16:13): Once born again by God's Spirit of life, his Spirit of truth begins to branch and guide us into all truth.

3. *Spirit of faith* (see 2 Corinthians 4:13): As our understanding continues to grow through the knowledge of God's truth, the Spirit of faith begins to strengthen our hearts with the confidence, patience, and boldness we need to follow Christ.

4. *Spirit of prophecy* (see Revelation 19:10): As our faith in the counsel of God's word increases, our understanding of the testimony of Jesus increases.

5. *Spirit of meekness* (see 1 Corinthians 4:21): As the testimony of Jesus increases within us, it develops the strength of his meekness within us. *Meekness is not weakness; meekness is controlled strength.*

6. *Spirit of grace* (see Hebrews 10:29): God's Spirit of grace magnifies this strength of God's meekness in our hearts by channeling his compassion, longsuffering, mercy, and gentleness through us.

7. *Spirit of glory* (see 1 Peter 4:14): As God's Spirit of grace matures within us, his Spirit of glory will shine from us. It will shine from our hearts and outwardly rest upon us, bringing the light of his love into the darkness of our world.

Ye are the light of the world. (Matthew 5:14)

From the moment we are implanted with the seed of God's word and are born again through eternal fertilization, the earnest of God's Spirit is birthed in our hearts—the Spirit of life.[193] It then continues to branch and grow until the full measure of God's nature is formed within us and we become a mature person in the stature and fullness of Christ. I believe Jesus was referencing this growth process when he recounted, "First the blade, then the ear, after that the full corn in the ear" (Mark 4:28).

That he would grant you, according to the riches of his glory,
to be strengthened with might by his Spirit in the inner man.

EPHESIANS 3:16

And other fell on good ground, and did yield fruit that sprang up and
increased; and brought forth, some thirty, and some sixty,
and some an hundred.

MARK 4:8

And the *fruit of righteousness* is sown in peace of them that
make peace.

JAMES 3:18, ITALICS ADDED

Section VIII—The Pattern's Forerunner

He, to rescue me from danger, interposed his precious blood.

ROBERT ROBINSON (1735–1790)

28

The Compounded Gift 🍃

*Jesus answered and said unto her, If thou knewest the gift of God,
and who it is that saith to thee, Give me to drink;
thou wouldest have asked of him, and he would have
given thee living water.*

JOHN 4:10

Painting the roof was beyond hot. I couldn't drink enough water. The searing heat of the midmorning sun on the hot rusty metal caused fumes from the dense epoxy to rise about me and take my breath away. The epoxy paint came in two containers, part A and part B. They worked in unison to create a chemical reaction for arresting the rust and preserving the metal while renewing the roof with the sound and vibrant color of a glistening new paint.

Much like epoxy, there are two parts to Scripture—the Old Testament and the New Testament—the old covenant of law and the new covenant of grace. The old covenant of law with its judgment is part A, and the new covenant of grace with its mercy is part B. In the searing heat of the Old Testament law, its judgments rise within us and makes us thirsty for the living waters of New Testament grace. Nothing can satisfy this thirst for righteousness like the abundance of mercy in God's gift of clemency toward man. The two covenants of law and grace work in unison to create a compound reaction for arresting sin and preserving our lives with the sound and vibrant color of a glistening new nature—the divine nature.

The old covenant with its many sacrifices and offerings for sin was God's schoolmaster to instruct us in the moral and just requirements of the law; the new covenant with its one sacrifice for sin met those moral and just requirements to set us free from the law's judgment and resulting condemnation.[194] Our knowledge of the law's demands for justice in the Old Testament didn't make us righteous like Christ, it just made us hungry and thirsty for the righteousness of him.[195]

God's old covenant of law was very much like a conditional contract, because it was based on our performance of God's commandments, but his new covenant of grace is a gift of clemency that's not based on our performance of the law because it's based on his Son's faithful performance of the law. And because God's grace is a gift, it is to be received with faith.

> Our Father has enabled us to be accepted in his beloved through his two-part plan of the law for learning and grace for pardoning.

By fulfilling the demands of the law that came against us in "covenant A," and then imputing his righteousness to us through mercy in "covenant B," our Father has quenched our thirst for righteousness and refreshed our hearts with a grant of absolution by which we can know the joy of his eternal salvation.[196] Our Father has enabled us to be accepted in his beloved through his two-part plan of the law for learning and grace for pardoning. I can see such a richness in God's clemency that it causes a searing heat to rise within me and take my breath away.

To the praise of the glory of his grace, wherein he hath made us *accepted in the beloved*. In whom we have redemption through his blood, the forgiveness of sins, according to the riches of his grace. (Ephesians 1:6–7, italics added)

Under the old covenant of law, animal sacrifices were imperfect offerings. They were precursors of good things to come and mere representations of what our forerunner would do to blend the requirements of the law—part A, with the better hope of mercy, part B, to perfect God's covenant of grace that ushers in the better hope. A hope by which we can draw nigh unto God with the confidence to boldly follow our forerunner.

> We needed a better sacrifice who could repair our breach and guarantee God's absolution.

The blood of animals could not meet the law's requirement of a breach for a breach, because they did not meet the law's just requirements of an equal or greater restitution. Neither could the sacrifice of animals give God the confidence to remove his veil so any man could come to him under the sovereign protection of a sacred blood covenant. They couldn't change man's nature, render him flawless, make him incorruptible, or raise him out of the grave to eternal life. Therefore, the world needed a better hope. We needed a better sacrifice who could repair our breach and guarantee God's absolution, so we could draw nigh unto God and live.

For the law made nothing perfect, but *the bringing in of a better hope did*; by the which we draw nigh unto God. (Hebrews 7:19, italics added)

Animals' blood was not the substance of God's promise to shield and reward us with his person, it couldn't be. Animals weren't equal to man, and they weren't the promised seed of Abraham, so they couldn't reconcile us to God on the hallowed grounds of agapao love.

They couldn't even shield us from the damage we do to ourselves as we grope through the shadows of Eden. The true substance of God's promise to shield and reward us through Abraham's seed was not manifested until Jesus was sent to meet the pattern's requirements as our atoning sacrifice and forerunner, and who would go before us to interpose his precious blood and secure our salvation.

> ...we violently took their lives to ease the pain of our violent actions.

Simply put, animal sacrifices covered the painful consequences of sin much like aspirin—they numbed the hurt until our wound could be healed by Jesus's stripes.[197] They couldn't heal the devastating effects of the sin virus in our hearts or repair our hearts from the wounds of our past, "For it is not possible that the blood of bulls and of goats should take away sins" (Hebrews 10:4).

True sacrifices must come from our hearts, not from animals who never willingly gave their lives for ours. On the contrary, we violently took their lives to ease the pain of our violent actions. Therefore, the national sacrifices under the old covenant of law had to be continually made year after year, because the painful deeds of our sin-infected hearts continued year after year.

> We owe a debt of appreciation to the many animals who stayed our final judgment for sin, but we owe our lives to Christ.

Unlike animals, Jesus's one sacrifice for sin met the full performance of love straight from the heart. His one offering for sin was so vastly superior to animal sacrifices that the author of Hebrews could assure us there is no need for another sacrifice, saying, "By one sacrifice he [Jesus] *has made perfect forever* those who are being *made holy*" (10:14, NIV, italics added).[198] Paul then went on to say, "If any man be in Christ, he is a new creature: old things are passed away; behold, all things are become new" (2 Corinthians 5:17). We owe a debt of appreciation to the many animals who stayed our final judgment for sin, but we owe our lives to Christ.

The story of God's Lamb is the greatest story ever told. The joy and sorrow of Calvary that purchased our pardon through grace captures the highest expression of agapao love. Our omniscient Father has lovingly allowed our hearts to experience the sorrow of sin and then he sent his Son to cleanse them, so he could sow our cleansed hearts with his seeds of love and prepare our souls for their resurgence from the dust. The blood of animals could not do this.

The sacrifice of animals never gave anyone the power of a sinless life, but they did help us to understand our need for it. They showed us we were too weak to walk where Jesus walked without divine intervention—too weak until God's mercy was mixed with our Messiah's faithfulness to create the compound expression of grace that galvanized God's new covenant. A blood covenant of unmerited favor that could arrest our sin and preserve our lives with a glistening new nature.

> The new covenant was based entirely on Jesus's satisfaction of justice and the Father's extension of mercy.

Jesus, our forerunner, was sent to mix God's mercy with a man's faithfulness and fulfill the law of love. He was sent to walk the pattern before us and establish God's new covenant of grace, so we would be accepted in the beloved the moment we arrive. The new covenant was based entirely on Jesus's satisfaction of justice and the Father's extension of mercy. How else could we become one with the high and lofty One who inhabits eternity? The One who will take our breath away in the searing heat of his glory?

Whom God hath set forth to be a propitiation *through faith in his blood*, to declare his righteousness for the remission of sins that are past, through the forbearance of God. (Romans 3:25, italics added)

For what the law could not do, in that it was weak through the flesh,
God sending his own Son in the likeness of sinful flesh,
and for sin, condemned sin in the flesh:
That the righteousness of the law might be fulfilled in us,
who walk not after the flesh, but after the Spirit.

ROMANS 8:3–4

For if that first covenant had been faultless,
then should no place have been sought for the second.

HEBREWS 8:7

But now Christ is risen from the dead, *and* has become the
firstfruits of those that have fallen asleep.
For since by man *came* death [the first Adam], by man also *came*
the resurrection of the dead [the last Adam].

1 CORINTHIANS 15:20–21, NKJV

29

The Blood Covenant 🍃

This is *the covenant that I will make with them* after those days,
saith the Lord, I will put my laws into their hearts, and in their
minds will I write them; And their sins and iniquities
will I remember no more.

HEBREWS 10:16–17, ITALICS ADDED

A covenant is not a contract—not even close. When I married in 1973, I thought of marriage as a conditional contract, almost like a business deal. For example, in a contract, an agreed-upon amount of money is exchanged for a desired item or service. Accordingly, I felt both parties had to perform in accordance with the terms of the agreement or the marriage could

> 🍃
> Take the covenant
> out of marriage, and
> all you have left is a
> weak social custom.

be nullified at will. So I willed it and we divorced. It took me years to finally learn that a marriage is not a contract but a covenant. It's a spiritual commitment made from the heart to give one's life to another. Take the covenant out of marriage, and all you have left is a weak social custom.

For this cause shall a man leave father and mother, and shall cleave to his wife: and they twain shall be one flesh? Wherefore they are no more twain, but one flesh. (Matthew 19:5–6)

In a conditional contract, both parties must perform their part of the agreement to meet its requirements. But a covenant is so much different. In a blood covenant both parties are responsible for the well-being of the other. This is the reason a blood covenant is the greatest of all covenants—*it is my life for your life and your life for mine.*

In a blood covenant, the stronger must shoulder the life of the weaker, because in such a covenant both parties have become one through an oath that is confessed as a pledge and sealed with a blood guarantee. The guarantee is often called a surety, which means it's the basis of confidence or security for the reliability of their oath. In a blood covenant, both parties pledge their oath to do whatever it takes to further each other's well-being, and then their oath is backed with their own life's blood or with the blood substitution of a designated sacrifice such as a lamb. Moses clarified the strength of blood to back a covenant when he told us "the life of the flesh is in the blood" (Leviticus 17:11). So to give a blood surety for a covenant oath is to back the oath with the covenantor's life—with all they've got.

> ...we are to govern ourselves by our oath to each other.

Therefore, when both parties give blood for their surety, they give the highest surety they can give. It becomes a binding guarantee that surpasses all other guarantees, because it is backed with their lives. Once we enter this highest of all covenants, we are no longer separate entities who are ruled by the whims and desires of our free will. Instead, we are to govern ourselves by our oath to each other.

In the case of the New Testament of grace, it's an incredible blood covenant between God and man that, as we are going to see, is backed with the amalgamated blood of God and man—the blood of God's Lamb. This New Testament covenant is essentially about God's life for man's[199] and man's life for God's. Take this covenant out of Scripture, and all you have left is a weak social religion.

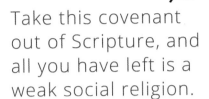

> Take this covenant out of Scripture, and all you have left is a weak social religion.

The New Testament is a blood covenant between God and man. It has been initiated by God the stronger who gave his oath of confession saying, whosoever believes in his Son shall not perish but shall have everlasting life (see John 3:16), and the surety for his oath is the blood of his Lamb.[200] But to enter God's covenant of grace and consummate the covenant with him, we must make an oath of confession too. Our oath of confession must be that Jesus is Lord, and the surety for our oath is also the blood of God's Lamb (see Romans 3:25–26). Paul reaffirmed the oath we must make when he wrote, "That if thou shalt confess with thy mouth the Lord Jesus, and shalt believe in thine heart that God hath raised him from the dead, thou shalt be saved. For with the heart man believeth unto righteousness; and with the mouth confession is made unto salvation" (Romans 10:9–10, italics added). Therefore, to enter into this covenant of grace with God we must believe in God's covenant sacrifice, confess he is Lord, and put our faith in

> Our oath of confession must be that Jesus is Lord, and the surety for our oath is also the blood of God's Lamb.

his blood for the covenant surety, and to keep from breaking our covenant oath, we must yield our will to his sovereign authority and back our talk with our walk.

But let's be transparent here, there are times when most of us have violated our oath[201] by not honoring our confession that Jesus is Lord, times when Christ the stronger had to shoulder our weaknesses as our mediator and advocate to help us toward the finish line. Personally speaking, faithfully yielding my will to Jesus as Lord is a work in progress that will probably challenge me for the rest of this life (see Ephesians 4:11–13).

> For the stronger to shield the weaker with his or her life is one of the most romantic glories of the sacred blood covenant.

For the stronger to shield the weaker with his or her life is one of the most romantic glories of the sacred blood covenant. In the case of God's covenant of grace with man, the true romance of the story is that Jesus has shouldered our weaknesses by shedding his blood to provide our covenant surety. Paul reaffirmed this when he wrote to the Roman church that God has set Jesus forth to be our propitiation through faith in his blood (3:25).

Jesus the stronger shouldered us the weaker with his atoning sacrifice, and then he gave his life's blood as the surety for the oaths of both parties—for the oath of God and the oath of man. Jesus carried the amalgamated bloodline of both covenantors in his veins, therefore, as the Son of God,[202] Jesus's blood was the qualified surety for God's oath to man, and as the Son of man,[203] his blood was the qualified surety for man's oath to God. So as the offspring of both God and man, Jesus's sacrifice provided the reliable surety for the oaths of both parties. Therefore, to initiate this new covenant, God had to put his faith in the Lamb's blood surety *to accept us beyond his veil,* just as we must put our faith in the Lamb's blood surety *to accept him beyond ours.*

To complete his mission to make us one, Jesus initiated the covenant by entering God's holiest place and sprinkling the blood of a man for God's acceptance of man, but to consummate the covenant, he must enter our holiest place to sprinkle the blood of God for our acceptance of God. This is why Jesus could say to all men, "Behold, I stand at the door, and knock: if any man hear my voice, and open the door, I will come in to him, and will sup with him, and he with me" (Revelation 3:20), and why Peter could say we are the "elect according to the foreknowledge of God the Father, through sanctification of the Spirit, unto obedience and *sprinkling of the blood of Jesus Christ*" (1 Peter 1:2, italics added). It is why the primary reason for Jesus's mission was to put God in us and us in God (see John 17:20–23).

> The primary reason for Jesus's mission was to put God in us and us in God.

Today the blood of Christ is available to every person in every nation because Jesus has shed his blood for all men—for the whole world. Therefore, whosoever will enter into this covenant of grace with a true heart and the full assurance of faith in Jesus's sacrifice will have their hearts sprinkled from an evil conscience by the blood of the everlasting covenant.[204] This is great news.

To Jesus the mediator of the new covenant, and to the blood of sprinkling. (Hebrews 12:24)

This cup is the new testament in my blood, which is shed for you.

LUKE 22:20

This is my blood of the New Testament, which is shed for many
for the remission of sins.

MATTHEW 26:28

Behold the Lamb of God, which taketh away the sin of the world.

JOHN 1:29

For when we were yet without strength, in due time
Christ died for the ungodly.

ROMANS 5:6

By so much was Jesus made a surety of a better testament.

HEBREWS 7:22

30

Preparing the Lamb 🌿

A body hast thou *prepared* me.

HEBREWS 10:5, ITALICS ADDED

When I was in junior high school, I raised some calves for a hobby. For several years, I bought dairy calves born from the union of two dissimilar seeds—the seed from a large beef bull such as an Angus was merged with the seed of a smaller dairy cow such as a Jersey. The dairy farmers said they implanted the seed of the larger beef bull into the smaller dairy cow to create a larger calf. They claimed a bigger calf caused the mother to produce a higher volume of milk.

Life is reproduced through the union of seeds, and sometimes it is modified through the union of dissimilar seeds. As with calves, we can achieve a desired result by engineering their conception, which is also true of human beings. We can engineer blood types and even modify the various traits of a child through seed selection, but this is just managing the natural selection processes. Through natural selection, our race has reproduced billions of individuals who are all unique. Born from the seeds of our natural parents, we have received the blood types, genetics, and various traits of our ancestors to make us the offspring we are today.

What about God? Can the alpha of life-giving spirits reproduce his nature in men through the union of dissimilar seeds? Of course he can. The incorruptible seed of God's word can be merged with the corruptible seed of man's flesh to reproduce a new order of flawless and incorruptible men—the order of life-giving spirits. These are men who are made in the likeness of Christ, the last Adam—the firstborn of many brethren.

John wrote that God joined the word and the flesh to generate Jesus's body and Spirit (see 1:14), and then Jesus said we must be born again of the same Spirit *to even see the kingdom of God* (see John 3:3). So this new order of life-giving spirits are a people who are born again by implanting God's word in the heart of their flesh to form the nature of Christ within them.

> We must be born of God's Spirit to confess from the heart that Jesus is Lord—to make our covenant oath.

When the seed of God's Spirit [his word] was joined with the seed of Mary's flesh to beget the last Adam, Jesus was being prepared to be the atoning sacrifice for the sins of man, the blood surety for the covenant oaths of God and man, and the forerunner of those who would follow his lead into the heavenly holy of holies. But again, we cannot follow Christ until God's Spirit is born within us and we are able to confess from our hearts that Jesus is Lord. Paul wrote, "*No man*...can say that Jesus is the Lord, but by the Holy Ghost" (1 Corinthians 12:3, italics added). No man! We must be born of God's Spirit to confess from the heart that *Jesus is Lord*—to make our covenant oath.

A Natural Analogy

For the invisible things of him from the creation of the world are clearly seen, *being understood by the things that are made*. (Romans 1:20, italics added)

When addressing the Roman church, Paul told us the invisible things of God are clearly understood by the things that are made. Again, this means spiritual things can be understood by observing natural things. So in the natural conception of a human embryo, we can gain a clearer understanding about the union of God's seed with Mary's and how this union of dissimilar seeds was merged to bring about the amalgamated blood of Christ.

At the very moment of human conception in a mother's womb, a total of forty-six chromosomes are joined together—twenty-three from the father's seed and twenty-three from the mother's. These chromosomes multiply and are found in the nucleus of every cell in the body, carrying the genetic information of both parents to determine the various traits of the child. By merging the seeds of the natural parents to create a new, living embryo, a child receives his or her life and becomes the heir of the combined genetics of the parents' blood alleles.

A blood allele is one of a pair of genes that appear at a particular location on a particular chromosome, and they influence their same characteristic in the child, such as blood type or color-blindness. Blood type is determined by the blood alleles (genes) inherited from the parents but not all blood types are equal, some are dominant while others are recessive. But not all genes are either dominant or recessive, some are co-dominant. Sometimes each allele in a gene pair carries equal weight and will show up as a combined characteristic.

For example, with some blood groups, the A allele is as strong as the B allele. So a person who receives a copy of A from one parent and a copy of B from the other parent can have a balanced blood group AB. This gives us probable insight into the prepared body and blood of Christ, who was made both the Son of God[205] and the Son of man.[206]

Just as we are heirs of our natural parents' genetics, Jesus is an heir of his parents too. The seeds of God the spiritual Father and Mary the natural mother were joined as one to procreate God's Lamb. He is the first union of God's word with man's flesh. So if in the likeness of Christ we are born again by receiving and implanting the seed of God's word in our hearts, then his word will be joined with our flesh through the union of dissimilar seeds. We will then possess the merged characteristics of God's spiritual genetics with our natural genetics to develop the heart and mind of Christ within us[207]—to be conformed to the image of God's Son.

> Just as we are heirs of our natural parents' genetics, Jesus is an heir of his parents too.

For whom he did foreknow, he also did predestinate to be *conformed to the image of his Son*, that he might be *the firstborn among many brethren*. (Romans 8:29, italics added)

The Last Adam

The last Adam *became* a life-giving spirit. (1 Corinthians 15:45, NKJV, italics added)

Jesus is the firstborn of life-giving spirits, the first of his kind in a body of flesh, the firstborn of many brethren. When the Spirit of God overshadowed the virgin's womb and conceived the holy child,[208] Jesus became the first flesh to be given the Spirit of God without measure.[209] This is why Jesus could say to Philip, "He that hath seen me hath seen the Father" (John 14:9).

Jesus was conceived through the union of dissimilar seeds,[210] so implanted within the chromosomes of his body and blood alleles were the combined genetics of God's seed and Mary's. By commingling the spiritual genetics in the seed of God's word with the natural genetics in Mary's seed, the last Adam was conceived in Mary's womb by the Holy Ghost to become the seed God had promised to Abraham, the seed by whom God would bless the world.[211]

The Holy Ghost shall come upon thee, and the power of the Highest shall overshadow thee: therefore also that holy thing which shall be born of thee [Mary] shall be called the *Son of God*. (Luke 1:35, italics added)

I doubt if anyone knows for sure if God's seed and man's seed were co-dominant, or if one was dominant and the other recessive. I could speculate that God's seed is dominant and man's recessive, seeing that our corruptible old nature must die[212] to develop the heart and mind of Christ within us.[213] But I could also speculate God's seed is co-dominant with man's, since the author of Hebrews called him a man when he wrote, "But this man [Jesus], after he had offered one sacrifice for sins forever, sat down on the right hand of God" (10:12).

Once the Holy Spirit overshadowed the virgin's womb and the last Adam's bloodline was formed,[214] the seed for the new order of a holy and righteous people was formed. God sparked his Spirit of life in the ovum of Mary to beget the new order of life-giving spirits—to beget the promised child. Isaiah foretold of this immaculate conception in Mary when he prophesied, "Behold, a virgin shall conceive, and bear a son, and shall call his name Immanuel" (7:14)—literally, "God with us" or "with us is God." Then Jesus spoke of the need for this immaculate conception in us when he told Nicodemus that we must be born again of the Spirit (see John 3:1–8).

The author of Hebrews declared that God prepared Jesus's body (see 10:5). The operative word in this text is *prepared*, in Greek, *katartizō*, meaning a body was prepared, and, of course, it was prepared to be the one sacrifice for our sins to be the blood surety for the everlasting covenant, the forerunner of all men into the holiest place of God, and the firstfruits of the resurrection.[215]

To *prepare* means to make ready beforehand for some purpose, use, or activity; to put in a proper state of mind; to work out the details of, to plan in advance. But the past tense *prepared* is even more explicit, meaning, it *has been done, it has been subjected* to a special process or treatment. Jesus's body was certainly prepared for our covenant sacrifice through the special process or treatment of joining two dissimilar seeds, which had never been joined before. In so doing, our Father engineered the righteous Seed for the kingdom of God by joining dissimilar seeds.

Jesus's binary blood was the first of its kind in the chronicles of man, but he was not the only man who would ever house the Spirit of God. We were all created to house the Spirit of God, as living temples, and now there are many who do. There are many who have been sealed with the earnest of God's Spirit (see 2 Corinthians 1:22).

Know ye not that ye are the temple of God, and that the Spirit of God dwelleth in you? (1 Corinthians 3:16)

Beloved, now are we *the sons of God*, and it doth not yet appear
what we shall be: but we know that, when he shall appear,
we shall be like him; for we shall see him as he is.

1 JOHN 3:2, ITALICS ADDED

For the earnest expectation of the creation eagerly waits
for the *revealing of the sons of God*.

ROMANS 8:19, NKJV, ITALICS ADDED

The wind blows where it wishes, and you hear the sound of it, but
cannot tell where it comes from and where it goes.
So is everyone who is born of the Spirit.

JOHN 3:8, NKJV, ITALICS ADDED

Having been born again, not of corruptible seed [flesh] but
incorruptible [Spirit], through the word of God
which lives and abides forever.

1 PETER 1:23, NKJV

31

Sealing the Covenant 🍃

For this is my [Jesus's] blood of the new testament, which is shed
for many for the remission of sins.

MATTHEW 26:28

D id God really prepare Christ to be the one and only sacrifice for
our sins? To be the One who would cleanse us from sin, impute
his righteousness to us, and provide us with the blood surety
for our New Testament oaths? The apostle John said yes when he told
us the Lamb was slain from the foundation of the world (Revelation
13:8). The author of Hebrews said yes when he wrote, "But this man
[Jesus], after he had offered one sacrifice for sins forever, sat down
on the right hand of God" (10:12). And Paul in his first letter to the
Corinthian church said yes when he wrote, "Christ died for our sins
according to the scriptures" (15:3). Even the prophet Isaiah said yes
when he declared there was coming a man who would be "wounded
for our transgressions" and "bruised for our iniquities," a man who
would bear our griefs and carry our sorrows, a man on whom the
Lord would place the iniquity of us all (see 53). Paul again confirms
this truth in his first letter to the Thessalonian church saying, "For
God hath not appointed us to wrath, but to obtain salvation by our
Lord Jesus Christ, who died for us, that, whether we wake or sleep, we
should live together with him" (5:9-10).

All things are of God, *who hath reconciled us to himself by Jesus Christ.* (2 Corinthians 5:18, italics added)

Jesus's body was our prepared sacrifice—period. His blood is our covenant surety—period. There are no ifs, ands, or buts about it. According to Scripture, which "cannot be broken" (John 10:35), Jesus is our Passover Lamb (1 Corinthians 5:7) who carried the bloodline of God and the bloodline of Adam to the altar of the cross, where he shouldered our sins by making the life-giving exchange of his life for ours and our lives for his. He became our sin, so we could become his righteousness.

The first Adam knocked us down by breaking the law of love, and then the last Adam picked us up by fulfilling the law of love. Our Creator God and Father used both Adams to build the strength of his love in our hearts and teach us about his great blessings on unity, so our longing for him would become just as intense as his longing for us.

> This incredible declaration is the very heart of the gospel message —the gospel truth.

God the Father chose us in Christ the Son before the foundation of the world, so we could be holy and blameless before him in love. This incredible declaration is the very heart of the gospel message—the gospel truth. Nothing else is important by comparison—nothing at all. Knowing this is the substance of our faith in the Lamb's blood. It is the substance of our hope in God's covenant of grace, in his promise to shield and reward us with his person, in his promise to resurrect us from the dust for face-to-face communion,[216] and that he would personally wipe the tears from our eyes (see Revelation 7:17, 21:4).

According as he hath chosen us in him [Christ] before the foundation of the world, that we should be *holy and without blame* before him in love. (Ephesians 1:4, italics added)

Paul reassures us in his letter to the Ephesian church that we were chosen in Christ before the world was (1:4), and the author of Hebrews reassures us that God's works were "finished from the foundation of the world" (4:3). So when we see informative phrases in the many biblical attestations about Christ, such as he was "foreordained before the foundation of the world," "slain from the foundation of the world," God has "chosen us in him from the foundation of the world," and "we are created in Christ Jesus...which God hath before ordained," they confirm without prejudice that Jesus the Christ, God's Lamb, was appointed to be our one and only sacrifice for sin long *before* Eden was planted and the first Adam fell. This is why the promises of Scripture can comfort our hearts with many awesome tidings such as, "For God sent not his Son into the world to condemn the world; but that the world through him might be saved" (John 3:17).

God's plan for our salvation began long before the first animal sacrifices were made in the garden of Eden, but Jesus's first step through the pattern's dynamics began in

> Violently nailing his body to the cross, the law's demands for breaching love were met with the full brutality of the consequences of that breach, so man's debt would be paid in full.

resurrect us from the dust for face-to-face[217] Then, over the next three days, he was delivered for our offenses, bruised for our iniquities, and then raised again for our justification.[218]

Approximately thirty-three years after the promised child was born in Bethlehem, the hour came for Jesus to be glorified.[219] At that appointed hour for his crucifixion, the hands of men unwittingly slew God's Lamb and poured out his blood for the covenant surety. Violently nailing his body to the cross, the law's demands for breaching love were met with the full brutality of the consequences of that breach, so man's debt would be paid in full.

Suspended high between the natural and spiritual worlds in full view of heaven and earth for all of creation to witness, the Lamb was slain and his blood was applied to the three essential places for removing our curse and consummating the covenant: *First*, it streamed down the cross to soak the ground and wither the curse on the earth.[220] *Second*, as the *Son of man*, Jesus sprinkled his blood in God's holiest place in the heavens, on and before God's mercy seat, to provide the blood surety for man's covenant oath and obtain our eternal redemption.[221] *Third and last*, as *the Son of God*, Jesus is sprinkling his blood surety in the hearts of those who will heed God's call and put their faith in his covenant sacrifice, so they can draw near to God by following Christ with a cleansed conscience, a surrendered heart, and the full assurance of faith.

> Through his faithful performance of agapao love, the life of the living God who loves man has been bestowed on the dying man who loves God.

Let us draw near with a true heart in full assurance of faith, having our hearts sprinkled from an evil conscience. (Hebrews 10:22)

At the unique intersection of Calvary's cross where the joy and sorrow of love were merged to secure our salvation, God's Lamb was brutally slain, his blood poured out for the covenant surety, and God's promise to shield and reward those who put their faith in his blood was set in perpetuity. Then our Supreme Creator, whose heart had ached for this union of beings from before the beginning of the world, ripped his veil from top to bottom with such a passionate fervor that it rocked the earth and cracked the rocks.

And, behold, the veil of the temple was rent in twain from the top to the bottom; and the earth did quake, and the rocks rent. (Matthew 27:51)

With the veil removed, our forerunner entered God's holiest place to sprinkle his blood on God's mercy seat, and initiate God's covenant with man. Then, as the mercy seat groaned and God's grace flowed freely, our rite of passage was granted to follow our forerunner to where no man had gone before.

By so much was Jesus made a surety of a better testament. (Hebrews 7:22)

Jesus was slain in the full view of *all* creation, between heaven and earth, *"for this thing was not done in a corner"* (Acts 26:26, italics added). Through his faithful performance of agapao love, the life of the living God who loves man has been bestowed on the dying man who loves God.[222] This beautiful genius of love's salvation will never fade away but will stand in perpetuity as God's gift of grace toward man—a grant of clemency that is backed with the blood-stained oath of God's everlasting covenant.[223]

> There had never been a hallowed man like Christ, a man who could give such a reliable surety for the New Testament oaths for men.

For by grace are ye saved [given life] through faith; and that not of yourselves: it is the gift of God. (Ephesians 2:8)

There had never been a hallowed man like Christ, a man who could give such a reliable surety for the New Testament oaths for men. Never was there a man like Christ Jesus, who was qualified to mediate such an extraordinary covenant for the union of dissimilar beings, a covenant that would stand in perpetuity on the might of his faithfulness alone. Never lived a man who could reconcile the living with the dead or the condemned with the just[224] on the strength of his faithfulness to love—not even close—until the man Christ Jesus became our conciliator for peace by fulfilling the whole law of love. Blessed be the name of the Lord.

Now the God of peace, that brought again from the dead
our Lord Jesus, that great shepherd of the sheep,
through the blood of the everlasting covenant,
Make you perfect in every good work.

HEBREWS 13:20

The Lord hath laid on him the iniquity of us all.

ISAIAH 53:6

The chastisement of our peace was upon him.

ISAIAH 53:5

Forasmuch as ye know that ye were not redeemed with corruptible
things, as silver and gold, from your vain conversation received by
tradition from your fathers; But with the precious blood of Christ,
as of a lamb without blemish and without spot.

1 PETER 1:18–19

Section IX—A Finished Work

For the stronger to shield the weaker with his life is one of the most romantic glories of the sacred blood covenant.

JOHNNY L. DUDLEY

32

The Joy of Unity 🌿

For Christ is not entered into the holy places made with hands [the earthly tabernacle or temple], which are the figures of the true; but into heaven itself, now *to appear in the presence of God for us.*

HEBREWS 9:24, ITALICS ADDED

In the tabernacle in the wilderness and in the temples in Jerusalem, God used animals to teach us how to follow our forerunner—the One who *has appeared* in the presence of God for us. For me, this sacrificing of animals for our instruction touches on the depth of God's great desire to be reconciled with us. Actually, God has used animals in many different ways to instruct us in the joys of unity.[225] So for me to learn a few things about those joys from the heart of my dog is not to surprising.

His name was Max. My friends said people who had moved out of their neighborhood abandoned him and left him to wander, so he needed a home—my home. They thought I was the right person to adopt him since I had plenty of room for him to romp and play, along with lakes and ponds for swimming. I knew Labs loved swimming, but I didn't need nor want the inconvenience of having to care for a dog. If I'd wanted one, a black Lab like Max would have been a great choice, but our hands were already full with three little boys.

Apparently, my friends disagreed. I soon realized how much they disagreed when I came home to a very young, black, short-haired canine tied to my front porch and barking as though I were the stranger. Little did I realize it was the first day of about a twelve-year romance. I loved that dog.

Max loved the ponds and the kids he swam with, and the kids loved him too. Between my two brothers and me, we had seven boys and five girls growing up together and they were all Max's friends. He acted as if our kids were his pups, and he never shied away from an adventure with any of us, except maybe sledding on Florida ice.

The day I took him over the edge of that steep, frozen spill bank of sand my dad had dredged from the lake was the first time I'd ever seen him shiver with reluctance. A rare north Florida ice storm had glazed the surface of the huge piles of sand, and we soon discovered that sliding down the ice on a round container lid was a lot of fun. But to wise old Max, tandem sliding was a bad idea.

After insisting he come aboard and squeezing him tightly while he groaned on my lap, the kids shoved me over the edge and away we went, twisting and turning and out of control, finally flipping over backward and cracking my neck. The recovery took a while for both of us, but eventually, after calling him again and again, Max limped slowly out of the thick bushes where he had run to hide from the scene of the crash. Perhaps his reluctance to come was because he thought I wanted to do it again. As for me, my sprained neck took weeks to heal, maybe months, and I still wonder if I might have broken it. I have also wondered, *how could any heart be as loving and forgiving as Max's?*

Sadly, Max didn't always recover. The day came when I had to scoop his frail, dysfunctional body into my arms and carry him to where he didn't want to go. My heart ached as he, being too old and too feeble to walk, fixed his eyes on mine for the very last time. I wept, and I wept hard.

I cannot imagine the turbulence in both Adam's and Eve's sinking hearts as they witnessed that first appalling consequence of sin—the death of at least two animals they had most certainly known and loved. The author of Genesis recorded, "Unto Adam also and to his wife did the Lord God make coats of skins, and clothed them" (Genesis 3:21). They must have been horrified at their first encounter with death.

To the dreadful dismay of Adam and Eve, the extreme consequences of their unfaithful hearts had begun a downward spiral toward the sting of death and permanence of the grave for them, their descendants, and for every creature on earth.[226] But God shed the blood of those animals they'd loved because of his great love for Adam, Eve, and us.

> To Adam and Eve, their situation must've seemed desperate, bleak, and hopeless, but it was not hopeless to God.

To Adam and Eve, their situation must've seemed desperate, bleak, and hopeless, but it was not hopeless to God. Our omniscient Creator who had already planned to provide us with an atoning sacrifice[227] and who declared the end from the beginning[228] understood that Adam's fall was a necessary step for creating us in Christ Jesus.

Following in the footsteps of the Levites, Jesus, our true High Priest, forerunner, and atoning sacrifice who was faithful to him that appointed him, accepted the curse of the law on his head when he accepted his crown of thorns (see Genesis 3:18, Mark 15:17). Then, after being crowned as the king of our curse, he paved our way to reconciliation with God because of God's extreme desire for reconciliation with us.

O death, where is thy sting? O grave, where is thy victory?
The sting of death is sin; and the strength of sin is the law.
But thanks be to God, which giveth us the victory
through our Lord Jesus Christ.

1 CORINTHIANS 15:55–57

Let us draw near with a true heart in full assurance of faith, having our
hearts sprinkled [with the blood of Christ] from an evil conscience.

HEBREWS 10:22

Wherefore, holy brethren, partakers of the heavenly calling, consider
the Apostle and High Priest of our profession, Christ Jesus;
Who was faithful to him that appointed him.

HEBREWS 3:1–2

33

Justice 🌿

For by one offering He has perfected forever those who are *being* sanctified.

HEBREWS 10:14, NKJV, ITALICS ADDED

The law is righteous, the law is holy, the law is just, the law is good (see Romans 7:12), and "by the law is the knowledge of sin" (Romans 3:20). Therefore, the law is not our problem, breaking the law is our problem. Violating the law of love is where sorrow was born and joy was lost.

Once the law of love was broken, justice stepped in to set things right. Justice is that part of the law that demands fair compensation for relational violations. It's within the law's responsibility to demand justice, because justice maintains what is good and holy by demanding a just recompense for relational violations. Without the power to demand a just recompense, the law would be futile and the earth would be lawless.

> ...the law is not our problem, breaking the law is our problem.

> Without the power to demand a just recompense, the law would be futile and the earth would be lawless.

When exercising its right to uphold justice, the law demands full restitution for our breaches against others, meaning full compensation with something of equal or greater value. This, of course, is why animals couldn't pay the debt for our sins, animals are not equal or greater than man.[229] Therefore, through the blood of animals, justice was only stayed until the last Adam would be sent to pay our debt in full and satisfy the demands of justice.

Think not that I am come to destroy the law, or the prophets: I am not come to destroy, but to fulfil. (Matthew 5:17).

God could have employed justice in Eden by exercising the full weight of the law on Adam and his bride, immediately demanding their final and eternal judgment, but he didn't. God loved them, and he knew mercy was superior to judgment. Our omniscient Father understood that a person's heart could be changed and even taught to love by being forgiven. A heart could both reap and learn the superior benefits of love

> ...full compensation with something of equal or greater value.

when mercy was exalted over judgment. Jesus went to Calvary to demonstrate that it is mercy, not justice, that releases the regenerative power of love.

Therefore, even though Adam suffered the huge consequences of being separated from God's face and physically dying at 930 years old, God postponed the eternal judgment of his soul, preserved his

> ...it is mercy, not justice, that releases the regenerative power of love.

bloodline, and redeemed a royal priesthood from his bloodline through his acts of mercy.

Our omniscient heavenly Father foreknew us, loved us, and foreordained us to share his glory before the world was, so he wasn't about to let us go down forever because of a childish choice our corruptible forefather was destined to make. As a devoted father who is focused on training his children in the way they should go, God launched our creation in Christ Jesus through the fall of Adam.[230]

God's workmanship in us has taken time, but it has been done right. The result is infinitely better than to have executed the full weight of eternal judgment in Eden. Isaiah proclaimed that God's ways and his thoughts are much higher than ours (see 55:8–9), which, according to the way God has engineered our development and redemption, is right on—completely accurate. If God is not willing that any should perish,[231] then I must conclude his higher plan has even brought redemption to the first Adam who lived before the flood.[232] The truth is, Adam needed to be created in Christ Jesus too.

Two Adams, Two Graves

It may have taken thousands of years of smoldering our hearts in the furnace of the earth, but God has accomplished his

> We were given over to die through the first Adam, so the last Adam could raise us up with a mind and heart like his own.

purpose for the reproduction of his offspring through the death of both Adams. We were given over to die through the first Adam, so the last Adam could raise us up with a mind and heart like his own.

The outcome of our creation in Christ Jesus is and always will be, God has purified our mettle through the shadows of Eden and taught us to love through the clemency of Calvary[233] by making us conformable to Jesus's death so we might be conformable to his life.

> God has purified our mettle through the shadows of Eden and taught us to love through the clemency of Calvary.

That I may know him, and the power of his resurrection, and the fellowship of his sufferings, being made *conformable unto his death*. (Philippians 3:10, italics added)

The Sorrow of Love

Jesus bore the cross alone, but he did not bear the sorrow alone. Through an infinitely greater sorrow of love than I could have ever known by Max's loss, God the Father carried God the Son to where no man wanted to go.[234] Surely the Roman cross loomed just as heavily before the eyes of our Father, as it did before the eyes of his Son. But the Father spared no expense and cut no corners in developing us, his paternal offspring, into the stature and fullness of Christ.

> Jesus bore the cross alone, but he did not bear the sorrow alone.

God the Father led God the Son to that infamous place of passion and tears where love and sorrow were merged. His mission being to transfer the burden of our sin virus onto the shoulders of his firstborn, so Jesus could take our virus to the grave. Then, as God's Lamb was being slain by those violent men who sent him to the grave, he gazed into the Father's eyes one last time before the Father, who could have no fellowship with sin, turned his face away.

> the Father spared no expense and cut no corners in developing us, his paternal offspring, into the stature and fullness of Christ.

Then we, being deceived and confused by the deceitful effects of the hideous sin virus, pierced God's Lamb with the viral hate and poured out the covenant blood. And I must conclude, if Jesus, the express image of God's person, wept at the death of Lazarus, I am sorely convinced our heavenly Father wept too, and wept hard.

Jesus yielded his body to be bound to the altar much like Isaac was bound on Mount Moriah. Only this time there would be no last-minute substitution, no ram in the thicket to replace the sacrifice, because Jesus was God's appointed sacrifice. Then, once the full weight of our pandemic virus was laid on his body, the hammer of justice fell hard on his hands and feet, the Lamb was slain, the altar was stained, and the earth quaked as it opened to receive the covenant blood. As I consider these historical events that were necessary to satisfy the justice of the law and create us in Christ Jesus, I have to wonder, *how could any heart be as loving and forgiving as God's?*

If the Son therefore shall make you free, ye shall be free indeed. (John 8:36)

Wherefore then serveth the law?
It was added because of transgressions, *till the seed (Christ)*
should come to whom the promise was made.

GALATIANS 3:19, ITALICS ADDED

Herein is love, not that we loved God, but that he loved us,
and sent his Son to be the propitiation for our sins.

1 JOHN 4:10

Unto him that loved us, and washed us from our sins in his own blood.

REVELATION 1:5

34

Chronicles 🍃

And the rest of the acts of Jeroboam, how he warred,
and how he reigned, behold, they are written
in the book of *the chronicles of the kings of Israel*.

1 KINGS 14:19, ITALICS ADDED

W e all have history. The events of our past are recorded in
our memories much like the events are recorded in the
chronicles of the kings. Like the records of how those kings
warred and reigned in their lives, our memories remind us of how we
have warred and reigned in ours. As we grow older, we may recall the
good and the bad, the victories and the defeats, especially at night
while lying restless in our beds.

The troubling truth for me is, not all of my memories are
precious—some are shameful and even despised. I wish those
embarrassing facts against me would go away and be blotted out
as though they had never happened, removed from my record
as far as the east is from the west. I thank God this will happen
for everyone who enters his covenant of grace through faith in
the blood of his Lamb. Once I understood the chronicles of
Christ and how he has warred and now reigns on my behalf, I
understood that I could ask him to do something very needful

and precious to me. I learned I could ask him to nail the sins of my past to his old rugged cross and blot them from my record.[235] So I asked him.

As far as the east is from the west, So far hath he removed our transgressions from us. (Psalm 103:12, ASV)

Today, after seventy years of writing my own chronicles on the memoirs of my heart, my need for the cleansing blood of Christ has become foremost to me. The only chronicles that really matter anymore are the chronicles of God's one sacrifice for sin, how Jesus has provided for my cleansing so he can present me faultless before the presence of God's glory, and how I am responding to his offer to come follow him and see God's face. Everything else pales in comparison.

And God shall wipe away all tears from their eyes. (Revelation 7:17)

The written record of the Old Testament rituals that foreshadowed the arrival and ministry of Christ, along with the precious promises in Scripture about how he advocates on my behalf as my mediator and counselor, are the only things that really matter to me now as I approach my journey's end. These precious promises shape my future and provide me with an inner confidence that brings peace to my soul, because of the victory Jesus won for my family and me on historic Mount Moriah.[236]

But thanks be to God, which giveth us the victory through our Lord Jesus Christ. (1 Corinthians 15:57)

Mount Moriah

Take now thy son, thine only son Isaac, whom thou lovest, and get thee into the *land of Moriah*; and offer him there for a burnt offering upon one of the mountains which I will tell thee of. (Genesis 22:2, italics added)

I can't imagine the turmoil in Abraham's heart when God asked him to go to a far-off place and sacrifice his son, *his darling*, through whom God had promised to bless the world. Abraham was sent to sacrifice his precious Isaac in the land of Moriah on the mountain called Moriah, where history records that Isaac was bound by his father and then delivered from harm by a substitute ram provided in his stead.[237] But Isaac's journey up the mountain with his father, Abraham, was only a shadow of the journey Jesus would make with his Father centuries later on that same mountain.[238] As an outcast by those he was sent to save, Jesus was taken to the outside of Jerusalem, the city that was built on historic Mount Moriah, and then bound in our stead so he could make the atoning sacrifice for our sins.[239]

> In the chronicles of history, Abraham offered Isaac on Mount Moriah, Jerusalem was built on Mount Moriah, Solomon's temple was built on Mount Moriah, God's prophets were slain on Mount Moriah, and God's Lamb was slain on Mount Moriah.

Then Solomon began to build the house of the Lord at Jerusalem in *mount Moriah*. (2 Chronicles 3:1, italics added)

In the chronicles of history, Abraham offered Isaac on Mount Moriah, Jerusalem was built on Mount Moriah, Solomon's temple was built on Mount Moriah, God's prophets were slain on Mount Moriah,[240] and God's Lamb was slain on Mount Moriah. Coincidence? By no means. These historical events have been carefully chronicled on the pages of the Holy Scripture because they mark the spot that God has ordained for our new beginnings. Mount Moriah is where the blood and water of regeneration flowed, so that innocence could be restored to those who follow Christ.

The Chronicles of the Sacrifice

In this book, *The Bridge of Hearts*, we have seen how the first blood sacrifices were made in Eden to protect our forefather's bloodline, but the sacrifices did not stop there. What continued after Eden is truly remarkable.

Individual patriarchs, such as Abel, Noah, Abraham, Isaac, and Jacob, carried the blood sacrifices forward. These patriarchs were in the messianic bloodline of Christ, and their individual sacrifices were given to cover their own transgressions until God brought forth the great nation of Israel from the iron furnace of Egypt.[241]

Once formed in Egypt's womb, God gave birth to that special nation by an extraordinary exodus through a sea of blood and water—the Red Sea (or reed sea), wherein the Egyptians attempting to follow were slain.[242] After delivering his chosen people through the Red Sea, the animal sacrifices went to a new level—a national level—they went from the individual sacrifices of the patriarchs to the national sacrifices of the Hebrew people to cover their sins until the promised Messiah would come and heal them.

As a new nation, Israel's sacrifices began on the naturally dry ground of the Sinai desert and ended some fifteen centuries later on the spiritually dry ground of religious tradition in the holy city of Jerusalem, the city of peace. When the appointed hour finally came to settle the debt for Adam's transgression,[243] God's Son, his appointed Lamb, paid our debt in full with his own blood.[244] Then, God ripped his veil to receive the only blood substitution that could completely reconcile us with God and deliver us from eternal judgment.

God was eager to restore the innocence of both Adams, the one who transgressed and the One who bore the transgression. This is why Paul could write to the Roman church and declare, "by *the offence of one* [the first Adam] judgment came upon *all men* to condemnation; even so by the *righteousness of one* [the last Adam] the free gift came upon *all men* unto justification of life" (5:18, italics added). The free gift of God's grace that came upon *all men* would certainly include *the first Adam*.

> God was eager to restore the innocence of both Adams, the one who transgressed and the One who bore the transgression.

By looking back through the record of events that set the stage for man's salvation and spiritual reformation, we should never forget that God gave an oath to bless the world through Abraham's seed, not through the seed of angels, but through a man who would come from Abraham's loins—Christ.[245] This is why Mary, Jesus's natural mother, was a descendant of Abraham's seed (see Luke 3:23–38).

Jesus could've taken on the incredible nature of angels and overwhelmed the world with power and glory so that all men would've instantly believed and pledged their allegiance,[246] but he didn't do this for a profound reason. Jesus took on the seed of Abraham because he was out to build a bridge of hearts, not a bridge of heads—to build a spiritual connection on the dynamics of agapao love, not on the dynamics of knowledge or superior strength. So to accomplish his Father's goal, Jesus went to the appointed place at the appointed time in the chronicles of man, to fulfill the oath God made to Abraham by fulfilling the oath he had made to God as shown below.

In burnt offerings and sacrifices for sin thou hast had no pleasure. Then said I [Jesus], *Lo, I come (in the volume of the book it is written of me,) to do thy will, O God.* (Hebrews 10:6–7, italics added)

Jesus, God's promised Messiah, was sent to fulfill his messianic oath to do God's will. His natural body was a seed from Mary who was a seed from Abraham's loins, and his unmeasured Spirit came from the seed of God's incorruptible word. His mission was to bless the world by shielding us from the eternal effects of the sin virus and rewarding us with the promised gains of God's person (see Genesis 15:1). Jesus accomplished his mission and blessed the whole world by bringing the blessing of Abraham to Jew and Gentile alike.[247] Then, once Jesus had shielded us from the everlasting effects of the sin virus and tendered the exceedingly great reward of God's person to us, God stopped the blood sacrifices.

For Christ entered not into a holy place made with hands, like in pattern to the true; but into heaven itself, now *to appear before the face of God for us*.

HEBREWS 9:24, ASV, ITALICS ADDED

Being justified freely by his grace through the redemption that is in Christ Jesus: Whom God hath set forth to be a propitiation *through faith in his blood*, to declare his righteousness for the remission of sins that are past, through the forbearance of God.

ROMANS 3:24–25, ITALICS ADDED

Fear not, Abram: I am thy shield, and thy exceeding great reward.

GENESIS 15:1

35

Stopping the Bleeding 🍃

But after that faith is come, we are no longer
under a schoolmaster.

GALATIANS 3:25

> Many people from the same generation who had witnessed the Lamb's crucifixion in 33 AD were still alive to witness the temple's destruction in 70 AD, only thirty-seven years after Jesus was crucified.

Jesus fulfilled his oath to do his Father's will by fulfilling the law of *love for us.*[248] Then the Father replaced the old "schoolmaster" of the law with the New Testament of grace, bringing about the speedy destruction of Jerusalem's temple to stop the shedding of blood. Many people from the same generation who had witnessed the Lamb's crucifixion in 33 AD were still alive to witness the temple's destruction in 70 AD, only thirty-seven years after Jesus was crucified.

Under the Roman general Titus, future emperor of the Flavian dynasty, the city of Jerusalem was laid siege and ransacked bringing about the temple's complete annihilation with not one stone left on the other. This fulfilled the prophecies of Christ about the future of the Jews and the temple as seen below.

The Prophecy of Christ Concerning the Jews and Jerusalem—Fulfilled in 70 AD

And they [the Jews] shall fall by the edge of the sword, and shall be led away captive into all nations: and Jerusalem shall be trodden down of the Gentiles, *until the times of the Gentiles be fulfilled.* (Luke 21:24, italics added)

The Prophecy of Christ Concerning the Temple—Also Fulfilled in 70 AD

There shall not be left here one stone upon another, *that shall not be thrown down.* (Matthew 24:2, italics added)

The Times of the Gentiles

Slaying God's Lamb ushered in a new age, the church age, the age of grace for our dying world. Jesus called it "the times of the Gentiles" (Luke 21:24). It began when Christ became our one sacrifice for sin, and it will end at God's appointed time for his Son to return and gather his people.

The fall of Jerusalem, the temple's destruction, and the dispersion of the surviving Jews into all nations gave rise to this Gentile age, ending the need to cover our pain and foreshadow the Christ with animal sacrifices. Christ had come and healed us with his stripes, so Jerusalem's once magnificent temple no longer served a purpose. It's not a coincidence that the same generation who crucified God's Lamb would see the complete destruction of the temple and the end of all sacrifices. It's his beloved Son's blood that was poured out on earth to heal and cleanse us, and it's his Son's blood that was accepted in the heavens for our justification and reconciliation.

Jesus fulfilled the righteous standard of *God's law* with the righteous standard of *God's love* to rouse the righteous standard of *God's mercy* and launch the new covenant of grace into perpetuity. The author of Hebrews gives record to the new covenant's superior advantage for men by saying, "He taketh away the first [*the Old Testament of law we could not keep*], that he may establish the second [*the New Testament of grace we could not earn*]" (10:9).

> Jesus fulfilled the righteous standard of God's law with the righteous standard of God's love to rouse the righteous standard of God's mercy and launch the new covenant of grace into perpetuity.

Jewish people don't perform animal sacrifices today. There has been no temple for the last two thousand years during the times of the Gentiles. The church age has become the age of God's clemency toward all those who accept the invitation to follow his Son, so there is no longer a need for a temple or an altar for animal sacrifices. Therefore, the Jews have not been able to uphold this ancient tradition of their fathers for the past two thousand years. The Messiah has come and given his life as a ransom for many, Jew and Gentile alike,[249] making our bodies the temple of God's Spirit and his cross our altar for cleansing.

> ...the Jews have not been able to uphold this ancient tradition of their fathers for the past two thousand years.

In my mind, the timing of the temple's destruction and the termination of its sacrifices are a sobering reality, a historical fact that validates the credibility of Jesus, his covenant sacrifice, and our faith in his amalgamated blood. It confirms beyond any shadow of a doubt that Jesus, our mediator, advocate, intercessor, and atoning sacrifice for sin, became our Bridge of Hearts by purchasing our rite of passage into the heart of God and establishing God's kingdom within us.[250]

> making our bodies the temple of God's Spirit and his cross our altar for cleansing.

The Holy Ghost hath made you overseers, to feed the church of God, *which he hath purchased with his own blood.* (Acts 20:28, italics added)

Unto him that loved us, and washed us from our sins in his own blood. (Revelation 1:5)

A Final Note

I thank God for the Jewish people and the horrendous labor pains they suffered to deliver the Christ child into our world so he could deliver us from the entrapments of this world.[251] They bore the torch of the coming Messiah until he came and unveiled the truth of God's love. The truth he revealed is that God's mercy rejoices against judgment, which, of course, made him the light of our world (see John 8:12). And now, for more than two thousand years since Jesus was sent, the Hebrew prophets have been silent.

God's Word has been sent, the recompense paid, the veil is torn, the gospel is preached, the brokenhearted are being healed, captives are being delivered, and Jesus has set at liberty many who were bruised (see Luke 4:18). Through the gut-wrenching chronicles of the Jews, mankind has been blessed with the greatest blessing this world has ever seen, Jesus, our Messiah. And now, for the last two thousand years, God has passed the torch to the Gentiles to carry the light of his love into all the reaches of the earth to establish his kingdom in the hearts of men. I am a Gentile, and I have written this book to proclaim God's love for you.

> I thank God for the Jewish people and the horrendous labor pains they suffered to deliver the Christ child into our world.

And hath made us kings and priests unto God and his Father; to him be glory and dominion for ever and ever. Amen.

REVELATION 1:6

Now unto him that is able to keep you from falling, and to *present you faultless* before the presence of his glory with exceeding joy.

JUDE 1:24, ITALICS ADDED

Behold, what manner of love the Father hath *bestowed upon us*, that we should be called *the sons of God*.

1 JOHN 3:1, ITALICS ADDED

A Song of My Life ✑

Sir, come hear a story, it's a song of my life,

Of a choice I have made that has caused me much strife.

From the joy of my Father I wandered away,

And my substance was wasted my gold turned to clay.

Yes, my substance was wasted my gold turned to clay.

My purse became empty, my friends wouldn't stay,

The life of my Father ebbed slowly away.

From the pit of transgression where I lay with the swine,

I longed in my spirit with my Father to dine.

Yes, I longed in my spirit with my Father to dine.

For my heart had been broken, my soul knew despair,

By the law I was dying, the grave called me there.

In great desperation, I cried from my place,

Please help me, my Father, extend me your grace.

Please help me, my Father, extend me your grace.

O, Jesus my savior, sweet Jesus my Lord,

My substance is wasted, I forgot your word.

I've sinned against heaven and now in thy sight,

Now I'm no longer worthy of the children of light.
No, I'm no longer worthy of the children of light.

From the heights of Mount Zion where the stones burn with fire,
The great King of Glory heard my desperate cry.
His compassion o'erflowed me like a river of life,
When he ran forth to meet me, to his servants he cried.
O, when he ran forth to meet me, to his servants he cried.

Go bring forth the best robe now, bring forth my ring,
Put shoes on his feet, cause the minstrels to sing.
Oh, bring forth the best robe now, bring forth my ring,
My son is come home, let the dancing begin.
Yea, my son is come home, let the dancing begin.

O, radiant Father who reigns from above,
When much is forgiven, then flows out much love.
My *heart's* overflowing with songs of sweet praise,
And my *mind* is consumed with the Ancient of Days,
Yea, my *soul* is athirst for the Ancient of Days,
Let my *strength* now be spent for the Ancient of Days.
For the Ancient of Days.

Johnny L. Dudley (1984)

About the Author 🍃

The author Johnny L. Dudley was born in Louisville, Kentucky, raised in Florida, and served in the Marine Corps in Vietnam. He is the father of three sons and is presently engaged as a real estate developer.

About the Publisher

Consecrated Press has been born from the lifelong discoveries and inspirations of Johnny L. Dudley.

The books published by Consecrated Press are meant to academically and spiritually educate, inform, challenge, and uplift the spirit of the teacher and the layman.

God's word and work are right in front of us; we just need to see it and embrace it.

To contact the author to arrange speaking engagements or to order multiple copies of this book, please visit our website:

consecratedpress.com

Endnotes

[1] And walk in love, as Christ also hath loved us, and hath given himself for us an offering and a sacrifice to God for a sweet smelling savour (Ephesians 5:2).

[2] And he saith unto me, Write, Blessed are they which are called unto the marriage supper of the Lamb (Revelation 19:9).

[3] Till we all come...unto a perfect man, unto the measure of the stature of the fulness of Christ (Ephesians 4:13).

[4] And it shall come to pass, that whosoever shall call on the name of the Lord shall be saved (Acts 2:21).

[5] And not many days after the younger son gathered all together, and took his journey into a far country, and there wasted his substance with riotous living (Luke 15:13).

[6] Whither the forerunner is for us entered, even Jesus, made an high priest for ever after the order of Melchisedec (Hebrews 6:20).

[7] Thou art worthy, O Lord, to receive glory and honour and power: for thou hast created all things, and for thy pleasure they are and were created (Revelation 4:11).

[8] For this people's heart is waxed gross, and their ears are dull of hearing, and their eyes they have closed; lest at any time they should see with their eyes, and hear with their ears, and should understand with their heart, and should be converted, and I should heal them (Matthew 13:15).

[9] He that overcometh shall inherit all things; and I will be his God, and he shall be my son (Revelation 21:7).

[10] Whosoever shall fall upon that stone shall be broken; but on whomsoever it shall fall, it will grind him to powder (Luke 20:18). And we know that all things work together for good to them that love God, to them who are the called according to his purpose (Romans 8:28).

¹¹ Woe unto you, scribes and Pharisees, hypocrites! for ye are like unto whited sepulchres, which indeed appear beautiful outward, but are within full of dead men's bones, and of all uncleanness (Matthew 23:27).

¹² For the grace of God that bringeth salvation hath appeared to all men, Teaching us that, denying ungodliness and worldly lusts, we should live soberly, righteously, and godly, in this present world (Titus 2:11–12).

¹³ To appoint unto them that mourn in Zion, to give unto them beauty for ashes, the oil of joy for mourning, the garment of praise for the spirit of heaviness; that they might be called trees of righteousness, the planting of the LORD, THAT HE MIGHT BE GLORIFIED (ISAIAH 61:3).

¹⁴ He that hath an ear, let him hear what the Spirit saith unto the churches; To him that overcometh will I give to eat of the tree of life, which is in the midst of the paradise of God (Revelation 2:7).

¹⁵ Knowing this, that the trying of your faith worketh patience. But let patience have her perfect work, that ye may be perfect and entire, wanting nothing (James 1:3–4). He that overcometh shall inherit all things; and I will be his God, and he shall be my son (Revelation 21:7).

¹⁶ For his anger endureth but a moment; in his favour is life: weeping may endure for a night, but joy cometh in the morning (Psalm 30:5).

¹⁷ Behold, how good and how pleasant it is for brethren to dwell together in unity! …for there [in the unity of the brethren] the LORD COMMANDED THE BLESSING, EVEN LIFE FOR EVERMORE (PSALM 133:1, 3).

¹⁸ Therefore the LORD GOD SENT HIM FORTH FROM THE GARDEN OF EDEN, TO TILL THE GROUND FROM WHENCE HE WAS TAKEN. SO HE DROVE OUT THE MAN (GENESIS 3:23–24).

¹⁹ My little children, of whom I travail in birth again until Christ be formed in you (Galatians 4:19).

²⁰ For thou hast created all things, and for thy pleasure they are and were created (Revelation 4:11).

²¹ For now we see through a glass, darkly; but then face to face: now I know in part; but then shall I know even as also I am known (1 Corinthians 13:12).

²² Whosoever is born of God doth not commit sin; for his seed remaineth in him: and he cannot sin, because he is born of God (1 John 3:9).

[23] So Adam gave names to all cattle, to the birds of the air, and to every beast of the field. But for Adam there was not found a helper comparable to him (Genesis 2:20, NKJV).

[24] For this *corruptible* must put on incorruption, and this mortal must put on immortality (1 Corinthians 15:53, italics added). Being born again, not of *corruptible seed* (1 Peter 1:23, italics added).

[25] And the Lord God said, it is not good that the man should be alone (Genesis 2:18).

[26] And they heard the voice of the Lord God walking in the garden in the cool of the day (Genesis 3:8).

[27] Note: The Greek language uses four different words to describe four kinds of love. They do this to avoid a misunderstanding of similarly written or spoken words. These are, storge—the natural or instinctual affection of family love; eros—a physical form of love shared between husband and wife: sensual or romantic; phileo—a strong affection between friends and companions; and best of all agapao. Agapao love is a sacrificial love that's not based on feeling, it's based on choice. It voluntarily suffers inconvenience, discomfort, and even death without expecting anything in return. In my own words, agapao love is the depths of love a person would die for.

[28] And to thy seed, which is Christ (Galatians 3:16). Wherefore then serveth the law? It was added because of transgressions, till the seed should come to whom the promise was made (Galatians 3:19).

[29] She was taken out of Man (Genesis 2:23).

[30] For this cause I bow my knees unto the Father of our Lord Jesus Christ, Of whom the whole family in heaven and earth is named (Ephesians 3:14).

[31] She shall be called Woman, because she was taken out of Man (Genesis 2:22).

[32] And the two shall become one flesh; so they are no longer two, but one flesh (Mark 10:8, NASB).

[33] And again, when he bringeth in the firstbegotten into the world, he saith, And let all the angels of God worship him (Hebrews 1:6).

[34] The seed is the word of God (Luke 8:11).

[35] Therefore if any man be in Christ, he is a new creature: old things are passed away; behold, all things are become new (2 Corinthians 5:17).

[36] For as the Father hath life in himself; so hath he given to the Son to have life in himself (John 5:26).

[37] For there are three that bear record in heaven, the Father, the Word, and the Holy Ghost: and these three are one (1 John 5:7).

[38] But exhort one another daily, while it is called "Today," lest any of you be hardened through the deceitfulness of sin (Hebrews 3:13, NKJV).

[39] For sin, taking occasion by the commandment, deceived me, and by it killed me (Romans 7:11, NKJV).

[40] Being born again, not of corruptible seed, but of incorruptible, by the word of God, which liveth and abideth for ever (1 Peter 1:23).

[41] Of his own will begat he us with the word of truth, that we should be a kind of firstfruits of his creatures (James 1:18).

[42] For the invisible things of him from the creation of the world are clearly seen, being understood by the things that are made, even his eternal power and Godhead; so that they are without excuse (Romans 1:20).

[43] And that ye put on the new man, which after God is created in righteousness and true holiness (Ephesians 4:24). And have put on the new man, which is renewed in knowledge after the image of him that created him (Colossians 3:10).

[44] Now he which stablisheth us with you in Christ, and hath anointed us, is God; Who hath also sealed us, and given the earnest of the Spirit in our hearts (2 Corinthians 1:21–22).

[45] For the law of the Spirit of life in Christ Jesus hath made me free from the law of sin and death (Romans 8:2). Now he which stablisheth us with you in Christ, and hath anointed us, is God; Who hath also sealed us, and given the earnest of the Spirit in our hearts (2 Corinthians 1:22, 5:5).

[46] Till we all come in the unity of the faith, and of the knowledge of the Son of God, unto a perfect man, unto the measure of the stature of the fulness of Christ (Ephesians 4:13).

[47] All flesh is as grass, and all the glory of man as the flower of the grass. The grass withers, and its flower falls away (1 Peter 1:24, NKJV).

[48] This matter is by the decree of the watchers, and the demand by the word of the holy ones: to the intent that the living may know that the most High ruleth in the kingdom of men, and giveth it to whomsoever he will, and setteth up over it the basest of men (Daniel 4:17, italics added).

[49] And to thy seed, which is Christ (Galatians 3:16). The kingdom of God cometh not with observation: Neither shall they say, Lo here! or, lo there! for, behold, the kingdom of God is within you (Luke 17:20–21).

[50] And the Word was made flesh, and dwelt among us, (and we beheld his glory, the glory as of the only begotten of the Father,) full of grace and truth (John 1:14).

[51] For what man knoweth the things of a man, save the spirit of man which is in him? even so the things of God knoweth no man, but the Spirit of God (1 Corinthians 2:11).

[52] And the angel answered and said unto her, The Holy Ghost shall come upon thee, and the power of the Highest shall overshadow thee: therefore also that holy thing which shall be born of thee shall be called the Son of God (Luke 1:35).

[53] Being born again, not of corruptible seed, but of incorruptible, by the word of God, which liveth and abideth for ever (1 Peter 1:22).

[54] So God created man in his own image, in the image of God created he him; male and female created he them (Genesis 1:27).

[55] Thou art my Son, this day have I begotten thee (Acts 13:33).

[56] In whom ye also are builded together for an habitation of God through the Spirit (Ephesians 2:22).

[57] For he whom God hath sent speaketh the words of God: for God giveth not the Spirit by measure unto him (John 3:34).

[58] The seed is the word of God (Luke 8:11). The sower soweth the word (Mark 4:14). So shall My word be that goes forth from My mouth; It shall not return to Me void, It shall not return to Me void, But it shall accomplish what I please, And it shall prosper in the thing for which I sent it (Isaiah 55:11).

[59] *The first Adam*; For whom he [God] did foreknow, he also did predestinate to be conformed to the image of his Son, that he might be the firstborn among many brethren (Romans 8:29). Who hath saved us, and called us with an holy calling, not according to our works, but according to his own purpose and grace, which was given us in Christ Jesus *before the world began* (2 Timothy 1:9, italics added). *The last Adam*; And now, O Father, glorify thou me with thine own self with the glory which I had with thee before the world was (John 17:5). Who verily was foreordained before the foundation of the world, but was manifest in these last times for you (1 Peter 1:20). The Lamb slain from the foundation of the world (Revelation 13:8).

[60] For we are also his offspring. Forasmuch then as we are the offspring of God, we ought not to think that the Godhead is like unto gold, or silver, or stone, graven by art and man's device (Acts 17:28–29).

[61] Above all, taking the shield of faith, wherewith ye shall be able to quench all the fiery darts of the wicked (Ephesians 6:16).

[62] For it was fitting for Him, for whom are all things and by whom are all things, in bringing many sons to glory, to make the captain of their salvation perfect through sufferings. For both He who sanctifies and those who are being sanctified are all of one, for which reason He is not ashamed to call them brethren (Hebrews 2:10–11, NKJV).

[63] And if children, then heirs; heirs of God, and joint-heirs with Christ; if so be that we suffer with him, that we may be also glorified together (Romans 8:17).

[64] But the very hairs of your head are all numbered (Matthew 10:30).

[65] Some good and well-known teachers have taught us that Adam's spirit actually died on the day he fell in Eden. But the Bible doesn't state, support, or even imply that unfounded claim. Adam was given the spirit of man when he was created, but not the Spirit of God; and the spirit of man is just as alive today as it was at the writing of the Old and New Testaments. Neither Adam's body, soul, nor spirit died immediately, he lived to be nine hundred and thirty years old as a living soul in a tabernacle of flesh, and he continued to beget sons and daughters with bodies, souls, and spirits like his own. *But what does time have to do with God?* It's not how long he lived that matters but that he was condemned to die. In the eyes of the everlasting One who inhabits eternity and is unaffected by time, Adam died immediately. Adam was dead the moment he broke the law of love, he became a dead man walking. In like manner, the Bible says we are all dead too, in the eyes of God, unless we are reconciled to him through the only redeemer he has sent from his bosom to cleanse and heal us. Sadly, through the processes of time, Adam's natural body did expire from the corrosion of his spiritual infection, but the grave truth is, the joy in his heart had died the moment he broke the law of love.

[66] And to make all men see what is the fellowship of the mystery, which from the beginning of the world hath been hid in God, who created all things by Jesus Christ (Ephesians 3:9).

[67] I am crucified with Christ: nevertheless I live; yet not I, but Christ liveth in me: and the life which I now live in the flesh I live by the faith of the Son of God, who loved me, and gave himself for me (Galatians 2:20).

[68] Whereby are given unto us exceeding great and precious promises: that by these ye might be partakers of the divine nature (2 Peter 1:4).

[69] And the Lord God formed man of the dust of the ground (Genesis 2:7).

[70] For no man ever yet hated his own flesh; but nourisheth and cherisheth it (Ephesians 5:29).

[71] And certain women , which had been healed of evil spirits and infirmities , Mary called Magdalene, out of whom went seven devils (Luke 8:2).

[72] Then took Mary a pound of ointment of spikenard very costly and anointed the feet of Jesus, and wiped his feet with her hair: and the house was filled with the odour of the ointment (John 12:3).

[73] Now when the Pharisee which had bidden him saw it, he spake within himself, saying, This man, if he were a prophet, would have known who and what manner of woman this is that toucheth him : for she is a sinner (Luke 7:39).

[74] The sacrifices of God are a broken spirit: a broken and a contrite heart, O God, thou wilt not despise (Psalm 51:17).

[75] For we know that if our earthly house of this tabernacle were dissolved, we have a building of God, an house not made with hands, eternal in the heavens. For in this we groan, earnestly desiring to be clothed upon with our house which is from heaven (2 Corinthians 5:1–2).

[76] For we that are in this tabernacle do groan, being burdened: not for that we would be unclothed, but clothed upon, that mortality might be swallowed up of life (2 Corinthians 5:4).

[77] And as it is appointed unto men once to die, but after this the judgment (Hebrews 9:27). Then shall the dust return to the earth as it was: and the spirit shall return unto God who gave it (Ecclesiastes 12:7).

[78] Furthermore we have had fathers of our flesh which corrected us, and we gave them reverence: shall we not much rather be in subjection unto the Father of spirits, and live? (Hebrews 12:9).

[79] All scripture is given by inspiration of God, and is profitable for doctrine, for reproof, for correction, for instruction in righteousness (2 Timothy 3:16).

[80] Again, the kingdom of heaven is like unto treasure hid in a field; the which when a man hath found, he hideth, and for joy thereof goeth and selleth all that he hath, and buyeth that field (Matthew 13:44). But seek ye first the kingdom of God, and his righteousness; and all these things shall be added unto you (Matthew 6:33).

[81] But we speak the wisdom of God in a mystery, even the hidden wisdom, which God ordained before the world unto our glory (1 Corinthians 2:7).

[82] I can of mine own self do nothing: as I hear, I judge: and my judgment is just; because I seek not mine own will, but the will of the Father which hath sent me (John 5:30).

[83] Even *the mystery which hath been hid from ages and from generations*, but now is made manifest to his saints: To whom God would make known what is the riches of the glory of this mystery among the Gentiles; which is Christ in you, the hope of glory (Colossians 1:26–27, italics added).

[84] Martha saith unto him, I know that he shall rise again in the resurrection at the last day (John 11:24).

[85] Jesus spoke these words, lifted up His eyes to heaven, and said: "Father, the hour has come (John 17:1, NKJV).

[86] And if children, then heirs; heirs of God, and joint-heirs with Christ; if so be that we suffer with him, that we may be also glorified together (Romans 8:17).

[87] To this end was I born, and for this cause came I into the world, that I should bear witness unto the truth (John 18:37).

[88] Who verily was foreordained before the foundation of the world, but was manifest in these last times for you (1 Peter 1:20).

[89] For whom he did foreknow, he also did predestinate to be conformed to the image of his Son, that he might be the firstborn among many brethren. Moreover whom he did predestinate, them he also called: and whom he called, them he also justified: and whom he justified, them he also glorified (Romans 8:29–30).

[90] According as he hath chosen us in him before the foundation of the world, that we should be holy and without blame before him in love (Ephesians 1:4).

[91] Thou art worthy, O Lord, to receive glory and honour and power: for thou hast created all things, and for thy pleasure they are and were created (Revelation 4:11). But as it is written, Eye hath not seen, nor ear heard, neither have entered into the heart of man, the things which God hath prepared for them that love him (1 Corinthians 2:9).

[92] Declaring the end from the beginning, and from ancient times the things that are not yet done, saying, My counsel shall stand, and I will do all my pleasure (Isaiah 46:10).

[93] Then God said, "Let Us make man in Our image, according to Our likeness; let them have dominion over the fish of the sea, over the birds of the air, and over the cattle, over all the earth and over every creeping thing that creeps on the earth (Genesis 1:26, NKJV). In the likeness of God made he him (Genesis 5:1).

[94] Today's wailing wall is a part of the Roman fort called the Antonia Fortress. Solomon's temple stood in the city of David near the Gihon spring.

[95] For what is a man profited, if he shall gain the whole world, and loose his own soul? Or what shall a man give in exchange for his soul? (Matthew 16:26).

[96] I will sit also upon the mount of the congregation, in the sides of the north (Isaiah 14:13).

[97] And he shewed me a pure river of water of life, clear as crystal, proceeding out of the throne of God and of the Lamb (Revelation 22:1).

[98] Sing praises to the Lord, which dwelleth in Zion (Psalm 9:11).

[99] Looking unto Jesus the author and finisher of our faith; who for the joy that was set before him endured the cross (Hebrews 12:2).

[100] My prayer is not for them alone. I pray also for those who will believe in me through their message, that all of them may be one, Father, just as you are in me and I am in you. May they also be in us (John 17:20–21).

[101] In the beginning was the Word, and the Word was with God, and the Word was God. The same was in the beginning with God. All things were made by him; and without him was not any thing made that was made (John 1:1–3).

[102] Shall I not visit for these things? saith the Lord: and shall not my soul be avenged on such a nation as this? (Jeremiah 5:9).

[103] That he would grant you, according to the riches of his glory, to be strengthened with might by his Spirit in the inner man (Ephesians 3:16). My flesh and my heart faileth: but God is the strength of my heart, and my portion for ever (Psalm 73:26).

[104] Marvel not that I said unto thee, Ye must be born again (John 3:7)

[105] For now we see through a glass, darkly; but then face to face: now I know in part; but then shall I know even as also I am known (1 Corinthians 13:12).

[106] Neither pray I for these alone, but for them also which shall believe on me through their word (John 17:20).

[107] But ye are a chosen generation, a royal priesthood (1 Peter 2:9).

[108] And there I will meet with thee, and I will commune with thee from above the mercy seat (Exodus 25:22).

[109] As it is written, There is none righteous, no, not one (Romans 3:10).

[110] My little children, of whom I travail in birth again until Christ be formed in you (Galatians 4:19).

[111] Whither the forerunner is for us entered, even Jesus (Hebrews 6:20).

[112] A minister of the sanctuary, and of the true tabernacle, which the Lord pitched, and not man (Hebrews 8:2).

[113] By which also he went and preached unto the spirits in prison; Which sometime were disobedient, when once the longsuffering of God waited in the days of Noah (1 Peter 3:19–20).

[114] In a moment, in the twinkling of an eye, at the last trump: for the trumpet shall sound, and the dead shall be raised incorruptible, and we shall be changed (1 Corinthians 15:52).

[115] Whom God hath set forth to be a propitiation through faith in his blood, to declare his righteousness for the remission of sins that are past, through the forbearance of God (Romans 3:25).

[116] Saying, Father, if thou be willing, remove this cup from me: nevertheless not my will, but thine, be done (Luke 22:42).

[117] And now, O Father, glorify thou me with thine own self with the glory which I had with thee before the world was (John 17:5).

[118] And about the ninth hour Jesus cried with a loud voice, saying, Eli, Eli, lama sabachthani? that is to say, My God, my God, why hast thou forsaken me? (Matthew 27:46).

[119] For he hath made him to be sin for us, who knew no sin; that we might be made the righteousness of God in him (2 Corinthians 5:21).

[120] According as his divine power hath given unto us all things that pertain unto life and godliness, through the knowledge of him that hath called us to glory and virtue (2 Peter 1:3).

[121] I have fought a good fight, I have finished my course, I have kept the faith: Henceforth there is laid up for me a crown of righteousness (2 Timothy 4:7).

[122] Let this mind be in you, which was also in Christ Jesus (Philippians 2:5). But we have the mind of Christ (1 Corinthians 2:16).

[123] Which shew the work of the law written in their hearts, their conscience also bearing witness, and their thoughts the mean while accusing or else excusing one another (Romans 2:15).

[124] See, saith he, that thou make all things according to the pattern shewed to thee in the mount (Hebrews 8:5).

[125] For we know that the law is spiritual: but I am carnal, sold under sin (Romans 7:14).

[126] Jesus said unto him, Thou shalt love the Lord thy God with all thy heart, and with all thy soul, and with all thy mind. This is the first and great commandment. And the second is like unto it, Thou shalt love thy neighbour as thyself. On these two commandments hang all the law and the prophets (Matthew 22: 37–40).

[127] O wretched man that I am! who shall deliver me from the body of this death? (Romans 7:24).

[128] Till we all come in the unity of the faith, and of the knowledge of the Son of God, unto a perfect man, unto the measure of the stature of the fulness of Christ (Ephesians 4:13). For this corruptible must put on incorruption, and this mortal must put on immortality (1 Corinthians 15:53).

[129] And He is the head of the body, the church, who is the beginning, the firstborn from the dead, that in all things He may have the preeminence (Colossians 1:18).

[130] The Spirit Himself bears witness with our spirit that we are children of God, and if children, then heirs—heirs of God and joint heirs with Christ, if indeed we suffer with Him, that *we may also be glorified together* (Romans 8:16–17).

[131] For we know that the law is spiritual: but I am carnal, sold under sin (Romans 7:14).

[132] And mount Sinai was altogether on a smoke, because the Lord descended upon it in fire: and the smoke thereof ascended as the smoke of a furnace, and the whole mount quaked greatly (Exodus 19:18).

[133] Then Solomon began to build the house of the Lord at Jerusalem in *mount Moriah* (2 Chronicles 3:1, italics added).

[134] Because the carnal mind is enmity against God: for it is not subject to the law of God, neither indeed can be (Romans 8:7).

[135] By whom we have received grace and apostleship, for obedience to the faith among all nations (Romans 1:5).

[136] For there is one God, and one mediator between God and men, the man Christ Jesus (1 Timothy 2:5).

[137] Thomas saith unto him, Lord, we know not whither thou goest; and how can we know the way? (John 14:5).

[138] For he [God] hath made him [Jesus] to be sin for us, who knew no sin; that we might be made the righteousness of God in him (2 Corinthians 5:21).

[139] And the Lord said unto Moses, Speak unto Aaron thy brother, that he come not at all times into the holy place within the vail before the mercy seat, which is upon the ark; that he die not: for I will appear in the cloud upon the mercy seat

(Leviticus 16:2). And he shall put the incense upon the fire before the Lord, that the cloud of the incense may cover the mercy seat that is upon the testimony, that he die not (Leviticus 16:13). The only known case of this happening is recorded in Leviticus 10:1–2, when the two Sons of Aaron were slain.

[140] And the very God of peace sanctify you wholly; and I pray God your whole spirit and soul and body be preserved blameless unto the coming of our Lord Jesus Christ (1 Timothy 5:23).

[141] And I will take away mine hand, and thou shalt see my back parts: but my face shall not be seen (Exodus 33:23).

[142] Behold my servant, whom I uphold; mine elect, in whom my soul delighteth (Isaiah 42:1). Now the just shall live by faith: but if any man draw back, my soul shall have no pleasure in him (Hebrews 10:38).

[143] God is a Spirit: and they that worship him must worship him in spirit and in truth (John 4:24).

[144] And so I tell you, every sin and blasphemy will be forgiven men, but blasphemy against the Spirit will not be forgiven. Anyone who speaks a word against the Son of Man will be forgiven, but anyone who speaks against the Holy Spirit will not be forgiven, either in this age or in the age to come (Matthew 12:31–32, NIV).

[145] And he made a vail of blue, and purple, and scarlet, and fine twined linen: with cherubims made he it of cunning work (Exodus 36:35). And he made an hanging for the tabernacle door of blue, and purple, and scarlet, and fine twined linen, of needlework (Exodus 36:37).

[146] Jesus answered and said unto her, If thou knewest the gift of God, and who it is that saith to thee, Give me to drink; thou wouldest have asked of him, and he would have given thee living water (John 4:10).

[147] For many are called, but few are chosen (Matthew 22:14).

[148] God is faithful, by whom ye were called unto the fellowship of his Son Jesus Christ our Lord (1 Corinthians 1:9). For many are called, but few are chosen (Matthew 22:14).

[149] Draw nigh to God, and he will draw nigh to you (James 4:8).

[150] Wherefore seeing we also are compassed about with so great a cloud of witnesses, let us lay aside every weight, and the sin which doth so easily beset us, and let us run with patience the race that is set before us (Hebrews 12:1).

[151] Enter ye in at the strait gate: for wide is the gate, and broad is the way, that leadeth to destruction, and many there be which go in thereat (Matthew 7:13).

[152] Trust in the Lord with all thine heart; and lean not unto thine own understanding (Proverbs 3:5).

[153] And the Lord spake unto Moses, saying, Thou shalt also make a laver of brass, and his foot also of brass, to wash withal: and thou shalt put it between the tabernacle of the congregation and the altar, and thou shalt put water therein. For Aaron and his sons shall wash their hands and their feet thereat (Exodus 30:17–19).

[154] That he might sanctify and cleanse it with the washing of water by the word (Ephesians 5:26).

[155] And he made the laver of brass, and the foot of it of brass, of the looking glasses of the women (Exodus 38:8).

[156] Thou shalt also make a laver of brass, and his foot also of brass, to wash withal: and thou shalt put it between the tabernacle of the congregation and the altar, and thou shalt put water therein. For Aaron and his sons shall wash their hands and their feet thereat (Exodus 30:18–19).

[157] And from Jesus Christ, who…washed us from our sins in his own blood (Revelation 1:5).

[158] That he [Jesus] might sanctify and cleanse it [the church] with the washing of water by the word (Ephesians 5:26).

[159] Now the parable is this: The seed is the word of God (Luke 8:11).

[160] In whom ye also are builded together for an habitation of God through the Spirit (Ephesians 2:22).

[161] But that on the good ground are they, which in an honest and good heart, having heard the word, keep it, and bring forth fruit with patience (Luke 8:15).

[162] My little children, of whom I travail in birth again until Christ be formed in you (Galatians 4:19).

[163] I will appear in the cloud upon the mercy seat (Leviticus 16:2).

[164] My little children, these things write I unto you, that ye sin not. And if any man sin, we have an advocate with the Father, Jesus Christ the righteous: And he is the propitiation for our sins: and not for ours only, but also for the sins of the whole world (1 John 2:1–2).

[165] For there is one God, and one mediator between God and men, the man Christ Jesus (1 Timothy 2:5).

[166] Wherefore, holy brethren, partakers of the heavenly calling, consider the Apostle and High Priest of our profession, Christ Jesus (Hebrews 3:1).

[167] I am the good shepherd: the good shepherd giveth his life for the sheep (John 10:11).

[168] Therefore doth my Father love me, because I lay down my life, that I might take it again. No man taketh it from me, but I lay it down of myself (John 10:17–18).

[169] Remember the words of the Lord Jesus, how he said, It is more blessed to give than to receive (Acts 20:35).

[170] He that believeth on me, as the scripture hath said, out of his belly shall flow rivers of living water (John 7:38).

[171] The sacrifices of God are a broken spirit: a broken and a contrite heart, O God, thou wilt not despise (Psalm 51:17).

[172] Narrow is the way, which leadeth unto life, and few there be that find it (Matthew 7:14).

[173] Love worketh no ill to his neighbour: therefore love is the fulfilling of the law (Romans 13:10).

[174] And again, when he bringeth in the firstbegotten into the world, he saith, And let all the angels of God worship him (Hebrews 1:6).

[175] And thou shalt put the mercy seat above upon the ark; and in the ark thou shalt put the testimony that I shall give thee (Exodus 25:21).

[176] And the sun was darkened, and the veil of the temple was rent in the midst (Luke 23:45).

[177] I will appear in the cloud upon the mercy seat (Leviticus 16:2).

[178] And thou shalt put it before the vail that is by the ark of the testimony [the Law], before the mercy seat that is over the testimony, where I will meet with thee (Exodus 30:6).

[179] Sacrifice and offering and burnt offerings and offering for sin thou wouldest not, neither hadst pleasure therein; which are offered by the law; Then said he, Lo, I come to do thy will, O God. He taketh away the first, that he may establish the second. By the which will we are sanctified through the offering of the body of Jesus Christ once for all (Hebrews 10:8–10).

[180] Therefore if thou bring thy gift to the altar, and there rememberest that thy brother hath ought against thee; Leave there thy gift before the altar, and go thy way; first be reconciled to thy brother, and then come and offer thy gift (Matthew 5:23–24).

[181] Note: The bread on the table was called the shewbread (pronounced "showbread"). Shewbread is called the *lechem panim*, the "bread of presence" or the "bread of faces." I like the bread of faces best, because it was to be eaten for communion face to face; in the face of, or mutual presence of, both God and man. It was also called "continual bread," because it was to remain before the face God always—at all times—eternally. The word *faces* is plural, because it represents God's intent to commune with man, face to face, through the Bread of Life—Jesus Christ. He is the bread of faces (see John 6:48–51) who brings us face to face with God.

[182] And the veil of the temple was rent in twain from the top to the bottom (Mark 15:38).

[183] They that are whole have no need of the physician, but they that are sick: I came not to call the righteous, but sinners to repentance (Mark 2:17).

[184] O Lord, the hope of Israel, all that forsake thee shall be ashamed, and they that depart from me shall be written in the earth, because they have forsaken the Lord, the fountain of living waters (Jeremiah 17:13). And the Spirit and the bride say, Come. And let him that heareth say, Come. And let him that is athirst come. And whosoever will, let him take the water of life freely (Revelation 22:17).

[185] And the publican, standing afar off, would not lift up so much as his eyes unto heaven, but smote upon his breast, saying, God be merciful to me a sinner (Luke 18:13). Come unto me, all ye that labour and are heavy laden, and I will give you rest (Matthew 11:28).

[186] But this man [Jesus], after he had offered one sacrifice for sins forever, sat down on the right hand of God (Hebrews 10:12).

[187] And he that sent me is with me: the Father hath not left me alone; for I do always those things that please him (John 8:29).

[188] Now therefore ye are no more strangers and foreigners, but fellow citizens with the saints, and of the household of God (Ephesians 2:19).

[189] Keep my commandments [miṣwâ; code of wisdom], and live; and my law as the apple of thine eye. Bind them upon thy fingers, write them upon the table of thine heart. Say unto wisdom, Thou art my sister (Proverbs 7:2–4).

[190] But other fell into good ground, and brought forth fruit, some an hundredfold, some sixtyfold, some thirtyfold (Matthew 13:8).

[191] Now he that hath wrought us for the selfsame thing is God, who also hath given unto us the earnest of the Spirit (2 Corinthians 5:5).

[192] For the fruit of the Spirit is in all goodness and righteousness and truth (Ephesians 5:9). But the fruit of the Spirit is love, joy, peace, longsuffering, gentleness, goodness, faith, Meekness, temperance: against such there is no law (Galatians 5:22).

[193] Now he which stablisheth us with you in Christ, and hath anointed us, is God; Who hath also sealed us, and given the earnest of the Spirit in our hearts (2 Corinthians 1:21–22). For the law of the Spirit of life in Christ Jesus hath made me free from the law of sin and death (Romans 8:2).

[194] There is therefore now no condemnation to them which are in Christ Jesus, who walk not after the flesh, but after the Spirit (Romans 8:1). Therefore as by the offence of one judgment came upon all men to condemnation; even so by the righteousness of one the free gift came upon all men unto justification of life (Romans 5:18).

[195] Wherefore the law was our schoolmaster to bring us unto Christ, that we might be justified by faith (Galatians 3:24). Blessed are they which do hunger and thirst after righteousness: for they shall be filled (Matthew 5:6).

[196] There is therefore now no condemnation to them which are in Christ Jesus, who walk not after the flesh, but after the Spirit (Romans 8:1).

[197] But he was wounded for our transgressions, he was bruised for our iniquities: the chastisement of our peace was upon him; and with his stripes we are healed (Isaiah 53:5).

[198] Where these have been forgiven, there is no longer any sacrifice for sin (Hebrews 10:18).

[199] Who gave himself for us, that he might redeem us from all iniquity (Titus 2:14).

[200] And looking upon Jesus as he walked, he saith, Behold the Lamb of God (John 1:36). The Lamb slain from the foundation of the world (Revelation 13:8).

[201] Watch and pray, that ye enter not into temptation: the spirit indeed is willing, but the flesh is weak (Matthew 26:41).

[202] Of a truth thou art the Son of God (Matthew 14:33).

[203] Whom do men say that I the Son of man am? (Matthew 16:13).

[204] Let us draw near with a true heart in full assurance of faith, having our hearts sprinkled from an evil conscience, and our bodies washed with pure water (Hebrews 10:22).

[205] And I saw, and bare record that this is the Son of God (John 1:34).

[206] For the Son of man is Lord even of the sabbath day (Matthew 12:8).

[207] Let this mind be in you which was also in Christ Jesus (Philippians 2:5).

[208] As a side note: Mary was in the lineage of David, so this also fulfilled God's promise to establish the seed of David on the throne forever. "And thine house and thy kingdom shall be established for ever before thee: thy throne shall be established forever" (2 Samuel 7:16). Also, in the book of the generation of Jesus Christ, the son of David, Jesus was also the son of Abraham (Matthew 1:1).

[209] For He whom God has sent speaks the words of God, for God does not give the Spirit by measure (John 3:34).

[210] We each inherit one blood type allele from our mother and one from our father, because each biological parent donates one of their two ABO alleles to their child (Richard B. Hallick, "ABO Blood Groups," University of Arizona, Tue., August 26, 1997).

[211] And in thy seed [Abraham's] shall all the nations of the earth be blessed (Genesis 22:18).

[212] Knowing this, that our old man is crucified with him, that the body of sin might be destroyed, that henceforth we should not serve sin (Romans 6:6). For to be carnally minded is death; but to be spiritually minded is life and peace (Romans 8:6).

[213] But we have the mind of Christ (1 Corinthians 2:16).

[214] Now to Abraham and his seed were the promises made. He saith not, And to seeds, as of many; but as of one, And to thy seed, which is Christ (Galatians 3:16).

[215] But now is Christ risen from the dead, and become the firstfruits of them that slept (1 Corinthians 15:20).

[216] For now we see through a glass, darkly; but then face to face: now I know in part; but then shall I know even as also I am known (1 Corinthians 13:12).

[217] Not my will, but thine (Luke 22:42).

[218] Delivered for our offences and was raised again for our justification (Romans 4:25).

[219] And Jesus answered them, saying, The hour is come, that the Son of man should be glorified (John 12:23).

[220] Cursed is the ground for thy sake; in sorrow shalt thou eat of it all the days of thy life (Genesis 3:17).

[221] Neither by the blood of goats and calves, but by his own blood he entered in once into the holy place, having obtained eternal redemption for us (Hebrews 9:12).

[222] Behold, what manner of love the Father hath bestowed upon us, that we should be called the sons of God (1 John 3:1). For Christ is the end of the law for righteousness to every one that believeth (Romans 10:4).

[223] Now the God of peace, that brought again from the dead our Lord Jesus, that great shepherd of the sheep, through the blood of the everlasting covenant (Hebrews 13:20).

[224] He that believeth on him [Jesus] is not condemned: but he that believeth not is condemned already (John 3:18).

[225] For the invisible things of him from the creation of the world are clearly seen, being understood by the things that are made (Romans 1:20).

[226] Because the creature itself also shall be delivered from the bondage of corruption into the glorious liberty of the children of God. For we know that the whole creation groaneth and travaileth in pain together until now (Romans 8:21–22).

[227] The Lamb slain from the foundation of the world (Revelation 13:8).

[228] Declaring the end from the beginning, and from ancient times the things that are not yet done, saying, My counsel shall stand, and I will do all my pleasure (Isaiah 46:10).

[229] For it is not possible that the blood of bulls and of goats should take away sins (Hebrews 10:4).

[230] And if children, then heirs; heirs of God, and joint-heirs with Christ; if so be that we suffer with him, that we may be also glorified together (Romans 8:17).

[231] The Lord is not slack concerning his promise, as some men count slackness; but is longsuffering to us-ward, not willing that any should perish, but that all should come to repentance (2 Peter 3:9).

[232] For Christ also hath once suffered for sins, the just for the unjust, that he might bring us to God, being put to death in the flesh, but quickened by the Spirit: By which also he went and preached unto the spirits in prison; Which sometime were disobedient, when once the longsuffering of God waited in the days of Noah, while the ark was a preparing (1 Peter 3:18–20).

[233] But to whom little is forgiven, the same loveth little (Luke 7:47).

[234] And he went a little further, and fell on his face, and prayed, saying, O my Father, if it be possible, let this cup pass from me: nevertheless not as I will, but as thou wilt (Matthew 26:39).

[235] Blotting out the handwriting of ordinances that was against us, which was contrary to us, and took it out of the way nailing it to his cross (Colossians 2:14).

[236] O death, where is thy sting? O grave, where is thy victory? (1 Corinthians 15:55). And having spoiled principalities and powers, he made a shew of them openly, triumphing over them in it (Colossians 2:15).

[237] Abraham lifted up his eyes, and looked, and behold behind him a ram caught in a thicket by his horns: and Abraham went and took the ram, and offered him up for a burnt offering in the stead of his son (Genesis 22:13).

[238] Take now thy son, thine only son Isaac, whom thou lovest, and get thee into the land of Moriah; and offer him there for a burnt offering upon one of the mountains which I will tell thee of (Genesis 22:2). And they came to the place which God had told him of; and Abraham built an altar there, and laid the wood in order, and bound Isaac his son, and laid him on the altar upon the wood (Genesis 22:9).

[239] Then the band and the captain and officers of the Jews took Jesus, and bound him (John 18:12). And he is the propitiation for our sins: and not for ours only, but also for the sins of the whole world (1 John 2:2).

[240] For it cannot be that a prophet perish out of Jerusalem (Luke 13:33).

[241] I brought them forth out of the land of Egypt, from the iron furnace (Jeremiah 11:4).

[242] The Egyptians armies that pursued Israel were slain in the Red Sea (see Exodus 14).

[243] And Jesus answered them, saying, The hour is come, that the Son of man should be glorified (John 12:23).

[244] Herein is love, not that we loved God, but that he loved us, and sent his Son to be the propitiation for our sins (1 John 4:10).

[245] The oath which he sware to our father Abraham (Luke 1:73). And to thy seed, which is Christ (Galatians 3:16).

[246] For verily he took not on him the nature of angels; but he took on him the seed of Abraham (Hebrews 2:16).

[247] That the blessing of Abraham might come on the Gentiles through Jesus Christ; that we might receive the promise of the Spirit through faith (Galatians 3:14).

[248] Think not that I am come to destroy the law, or the prophets: I am not come to destroy, but to fulfil (Matthew 5:17).

[249] For even the Son of man came not to be ministered unto, but to minister, and to give his life a ransom for many (Mark 10:45).

[250] The kingdom of God is within you (Luke 17:21).

[251] Love not the world, neither the things that are in the world. If any man love the world, the love of the Father is not in him (1 John 2:15).